A CAT & MOUSE AFFAIR
Exploring Sustainable Measures of Resolving the Vendor-Local Authority Conflict:

A Case of Marondera Municipality, Zimbabwe

Bruno Shora

Mwanaka Media and Publishing Pvt Ltd,
ChitungwizaZimbabwe

*

Creativity, Wisdom and Beauty

Publisher:

Mmap

Mwanaka Media and Publishing Pvt Ltd

24 Svosve Road, Zengeza 1

ChitungwizaZimbabwe

mwanaka@yahoo.com

https//mwanakamediaandpublishing.weebly.com

Distributed in and outside N. America by African Books Collective

orders@africanbookscollective.com

www.africanbookscollective.com

ISBN: 978-0-7974-9644-6

EAN: 9780797496446

© Bruno Shora 2018

DISCLAIMER

All views expressed in this publication are those of the author and do not
necessarily reflect those of *Mmap*

ACKNOWLEDGEMENTS

I salute Professor Pamela Machakanja of Africa University for thoroughly and diligently reviewing the book. Heartfelt gratitude to the Municipality of Marondera for granting permission to conduct the study in their area of jurisdiction. The supervision and direction of Professor B. Mapuranga was one of a kind. Technical advice from Mr F. Sadomba and Professor Musingafe proved worthy. I am also grateful to the Zimbabwe Academic and Non-Fiction Authors Association (ZANA), to which I am a member. The following also made valid contributions in one way or the other; Mrs.Rugonye, Mr Chimonyo, Professor Bukaliya, Apostle J. Muguraguri, Mr J. Lemekani, the late Mr S. Mtamba (may his dear soul rest in peace), Mrs D. MatemboShora and various research participants and colleagues who took part in this study. Thank you Trevor Shora for the finances.

LIST OF ACRONYMS

CBD – Central Business District
ESAP- Economic Structural Adjustment Program
NGO – Non Governmental Organisation
MDC- Movement for Democratic Change
SMEs- Small to Medium Scale Entrepreneurs
ZANU PF-Zimbabwe African National Union Patriotic Front

Definition of Terms

Conflict Resolution - a variety of approaches aimed at terminating conflict through the constructive solving of problems.

Local Authority – a group of officials responsible for the management and service provision of a particular geographical area which is not at national level.

Sustainable Measures –practical measures which can effectively prevail for some time.

Vendor-may refer to one who trades at stalls such as kiosk, one who operates from semi-fixed stalls, like folding tables, crates, collapsible stands, or wheeled push carts that are removed from the streets and stored overnight, one who sells from fixed locations without a stall structure, displaying merchandise on cloth or plastic sheets or mobile vendors who walk or bicycle through the streets selling.

CONTENTS

PREFACE

Following a study conducted as from February 2016, this book sought to explore sustainable measures of resolving the vendor-local authority conflict with special reference to Marondera Municipality. The book thus aimed to find means of promoting citizen participation in local governance, to win vendor compliance with the municipality's by-laws and also to explore the possibility of coming up with a vending policy for the town of Marondera, that which would promote a win-win situation for all the affected parties.

The target population comprised of vendors in and around the Central Business District, municipal officials and members of the civic society. In this regard, the intended beneficiaries of this book include entrepreneurs, vendors included, the civic society, students of various related disciplines (Peace and Conflict Resolution Studies, Development Studies, Rural and Urban Planning, etc) the policy maker, in the form of local municipalities and the Central Government.

The book demonstrates that sporadic raids on vendors by municipal police are still taking place. Vendors are willing to be designated reasonable places to operate from.

The registration/license fee is beyond reach of many vendors.

Almost all vendors prefer to trade in the Central Business District. There are no reliable credit lines for vendors in Marondera. The majority of street vendors do not have any form of social security. The majority of the street vendors indicated that the municipality does not or did not consult them before making any major decision. Ninety percent of the street vendors contacted were not registered. There is no vendors' policy drawn for the town of Marondera. Although the by-laws need to be refreshed, they are not the root cause of the conflict. There is a serious mistrust, lack of co-ordination and cooperation amongst vendors and the local authority. There is an absence of a strong, effective and vibrant civic society in Marondera.

As recommendations, there is an urgent need to adopt a third party intervention initiative in this vendor-local authority conflict. Citizen participation should be heightened. The municipality needs to do some awareness campaigns and conscientise vendors on the registration process. License fees need to be lowered so that they become commensurate with the currently prevailing harsh economic situation. There is a need to help establish strong effective civic society groups. In this regard, vendors need to be assisted so that they get organized and establish some vendors' associations which amongst other things will speak on their behalf. A three tier task force, comprising of vendors, the Municipality of Marondera and the civic society needs to be set up to ensure that all issues to do with vending and local governance are well coordinated, well implemented, well monitored and well evaluated so that mutual cooperation, trust and confidence building is achieved. The task force should go ahead and draft a vendor's policy for the Municipality of Marondera, which will exhaust all issues of interest, difficulty and concern in as far as vending is concerned. The municipality also may explore the use of vending machines as a way of decongesting the town.

CHAPTER 1:

THE PROBLEM AND ITS SETTING

Background of the vendor-local authority conflict

The relationship existing between vendors and local authorities (municipalities) has been reminiscent of a "cat and mouse" affair with neither of the parties realizing that they can make good use of each other. This is despite the fact that studies have actually shown that when urban management policies allow vendors to conduct their trade, there is a positive impact and results on several fronts such as on poverty, empowerment, entrepreneurship, social mobility, peace and order, (Kusakabe, 2006).

The net effect of such a state of affairs has been some bouts of violent clashes, some of which were near fatal. Consequently, on numerous occasions, members of both conflicting parties have appeared before courts of law. Reference can also be made to the case of State vs. Raymond Gova, CRB 2065/15 at Marondera Magistrates Court wherein the said accused person was charged for having assaulted a municipal police officer in one of the many clashes. The disruption of smooth normal business life has been a common feature.

The Municipality harbours a genuine concern, that those whom they have termed "illegal" vendors have caused a menace in the Central Business District (CBD) through haphazardly selling all sorts of stuff ranging from food, farm produce, and hardware to clothes at undesignated points of sale. This has not only posed a health hazard time bomb but has also irritatingly interfered with human and road traffic. On the other hand, vendors are of the opinion that through indigenization initiatives, which the current government is seriously advocating for at whatever cost, they ought to freely share the trading space particularly in the Central Business District, which has been mostly a reserve of the well-to do, and in which business is most lucrative than any other part of the town. Actually, Kusakabe (2006) also argues that in many countries, urban space tends to be a highly political issue involving many interests. Brown (2006) also added much to the debate as he was quoted alluding to the fact that in reality, there is no shortage of urban public space, as some critics may want to portray, but rather, the most profitable locations to trade are at the busiest locations where competition for space is active (Sarmiento, 2015, Zhuwawo, 2015, Harrison and McVey, 1997 and Yankson, 2000 in Ayeh).

It would also appear that vending has become the only viable source of living for most ordinary citizens who have not made it into farming or into mainstream employment and formal business sectors which in actual fact are crumbling as the economy is in its doldrums. In another survey, 88.3% of vendors indicated that street enterprise was their sole source of income, (Njaya, 2012).

All this testifies to the fact that a conflict is at hand. Sustainable measures of resolving, or at least managing the conflict ought to be explored. However, vendor-local authority conflicts are not something peculiar to the society in question only, but they have been a cause for concern globally, continentally, regionally, nationally and locally according to Cheema (2011) and Anetor (2015).

Back home, in Zimbabwe, there is no doubt that such a conflict is at hand and that it is very current as it has even made headlines in the mainstream media. For instance, *Harare vendors in suicidal war,* The

2

Herald, Tuesday 17 November 2015, *1 500 Mbare Traders face eviction,* NewsdzeZimbabwe of the 14th of February 2016, *Council U-turns on Mbare evictions,* NewsdzeZimbabwe of the 17th of February 2016, *Teargas as cops break vendors demo, arrest leaders,* New Zimbabwe of the 15th of July 2016, *We will drive out vendors: Harare Council,* NewsdzeZimbabwe of the 27th of November 2017 and *ITUC censures Mugabe over vendors, says crackdown on street commerce in violation of ILO laws,* New Zimbabwe of the 23rd of October 2017, etc. All this evidence demonstrates that the vendor-local authority conflict has been topical in Zimbabwe's major cities and towns, Marondera included.

But where and when did all this start from? There has been a general assumption or rather a matter of fact that the former colonial master, Britain, made laws which were restrictive and anti-black majority whilst ensuring that there was a separate development which had a bias towards the white minority community. Central Business Districts had rights of admission reserved with a few blacks who formed cheap labour only finding their way along the likes of Salisbury's First Street and other Business Districts, but not without some conditions.

One would assume that the above situation came to an end with the attainment of Independence in 1980. It indeed came to an end, but to an extent. In this regard, Dube and Chirisa (2012: 17) made a fascinating observation to the effect that "years after colonialism, there is still the perpetuation of the colonial legislation and in some cases even draconic restrictions". Well the validity of such a claim and the by-laws in question will certainly be reviewed in this book, but the gist of their input is that there is a general feeling that the trading space particularly in the urban and Central Business Districts is not evenly shared, hence it has become a contested space.

Njaya (2014), whilst making reference to Harare Metropolitan Province observed that the major problem seemed to be the city's master plan (designed during the colonial period) which did not allocate space to vendors as town planners blindly replicated the western concept of marketing which ignored Zimbabwean traditions. The same can also be noted to be true in the case of Marondera.

To further compound the situation, the government and general populace got choked with the adverse effects of the International Monetary Fund and World Bank-advised Economic Structural Adjustment Program (ESAP) which in the early 90s saw companies closing, the majority of workers getting retrenched and the standard of living dropping whilst the cost of living escalated. It is upon this background that the government then decided to relax some of the colonial laws through Statutory Instrument (SI) 216 of 1994 as reported by Dube and Chirisa (2012) who also quoted Tibaijuka (2005) and Vambe (2008). They further asserted that such a move was aimed at allowing the existence of the informal sector activities like flea markets, stalls, shacks and home industries by special consent.

Interestingly, this is the situation which led some critics to describe Zimbabwe's economy as a flea market economy. As time progressed the sector also came to be recognized in a more dignified manner or sector, the Small to Medium scale Entrepreneurs (SMEs). Well, this can be seen as the window through which city vending also found its way in Zimbabwe, Marondera included. Apparently, when flea markets were introduced in the early 1990s, trading was restricted to weekends but today, they are now in place almost round the clock, (Njaya, 2014).

One may also need to appreciate that this current vendor-local authority conflict in Marondera is not a new phenomenon, but dates backs about 10 years ago, when a near similar conflict began manifesting itself at national level. Dube and Chirisa (2012:17) are puzzled by the fact that "about a decade later (after the passing of SI 216 of 1994), the (vendor/informal) sector was still being labelled as trouble-causing to the economy" (Vambe 2008). Thus in May 2005, the same Zimbabwean government that enacted SI 216 of 1994 embarked on a clean-up campaign dubbed Operation Restore Order or Operation *Murambatsvina*, (Vambe 2008, Tibaijuka 2005). Skinner (2008) found such an operation to be the largest scale, and possibly the most violent eviction of street traders in the continent in the last decade. This period can safely be marked as a period when a serious vendor-local authority conflict began,such that, to borrow the words of B. W Anderson, it was a microcosm of the macrocosm as the same scenario also prevailed in local authorities such as Marondera. Illegal structures were demolished. Illegal vending sites were also destroyed.

Whilst the government's efforts were commendable, especially to come up with a housing project dubbed *Operation Garikai/Hlalani Kuhle,* so as to cover up the mess.From a human rights perspective, it would appear no viable, sustainable policy was then drawn up to address the issue of vending, besides allocating vending sites far much away from where business is lucrative. As a result, in less than a decade after Operation Murambatsvina of 2005, the informal sector, particularly vending, resurrected, re-emerged and actually became more resistant. It is therefore apparently clear as to how this conflict originated and there is need to find an amicable way of peacefully resolving such a conflict, (Chirisa and Dube 2012).

Therefore, in Marondera, a stalemate has been reached in the vendor-local authority conflict. Vendors, for some reasons, have vowed not to retreat from the so-called undesignated points of sale.

The municipal police is not giving up its fight against vendors in a bid to ensure that they are driven out of the Central Business District and its surrounding areas. More often than not, this has resulted in chaotic ugly scenes as the two warring parties clash more often than not.

A good fraction of the vending community either works for extended hours into the night or some of them actually assume duty at night and the reasons are that during this period of time, by-law enforcement agents will not be active. Instead, they would also have joined the market force during such a peak hour as the majority of people will be finding their way to their homes and they need to carry some commodities with them. Some customers who prefer to shop in formal supermarkets find it a mammoth task to manoeuvre in and out of the supermarkets as some vendors have positioned themselves just a step away from shop entrances. This has not only posed public disorder but to an extent, it has also posed a social and security threat which has got a potential of cascading into all other provinces especially if we take into account the fact that the vendor-local authority crisis is usually getting hi-jacked by several divergent political elements with differing interests, something which is not surprising when considering the nature of local governance which somehow is political.

The *ZANU P F –MDC* politicking is a typical example. The staff reporter of New Zimbabwe on 14 June 2016 published a news article titled *ZANU P F prepares for 2018 polls, takes campaign to Harare vendors*. In a related situation in Harare, Njaya(2012) was informed that there was a partisan allocation of flea markets sites as well as selection of vendors where certain areas were known to be for either *ZANU P F or MDC-T*. Some unruly elements have also capitalized on the situation by engaging in illegal and fraudulent activities such as defrauding unsuspecting customers and also selling illegal commodities such as dagga, locally known as *mbanje*, illicit beer and liquor such as *zed, kenge, klango* and *musombodia* and also the sale of untested and unapproved herbs, charms, concoctions (*guchu*) and body lotions thereby posing a serious threat and danger to public health.

In addition to that, vendors display their merchandise in front of licensed and tax-paying shops. Vendors' garbage cause an unsightly urban vista. There is also a hazardous environment which is caused by an absence of water and sanitation at some vending sites. Street vending at times obstructs and defeat the course of justice and the maintenance of law and order as some of the traders harbor criminals or criminal intents. There is also lots of noise pollution as vendors often advertise by loud cries and chants so as to attract the attention of customers, (Njaya, 2014). All this can justify why the local authorities feels they are compelled, if not mandated to regulate urban vending. It therefore becomes apparent that indeed a conflict of some sort is at stake. It is such a background which prompted the author to explore sustainable measures of resolving the vendor-local authority conflict in Marondera.

Marondera Town

The investigation of the nature of the conflict pitting vendors and the local authorities was narrowed and limited to the issue of trading space and factors surrounding it. It is such parameters which formed the boundaries of this book. Marondera is a watershed town located towards the eastern side of Zimbabwe covering a total area of about 3800 hectares. It would have been practically impossible with limited resources to survey a much wider area. Essentially, this book focused on Marondera's Central Business District which in actual fact is the epicenter of the conflict in question, covering about 40 hectares (see map over-leaf).

The illustration below shows the map of Marondera Central Business District

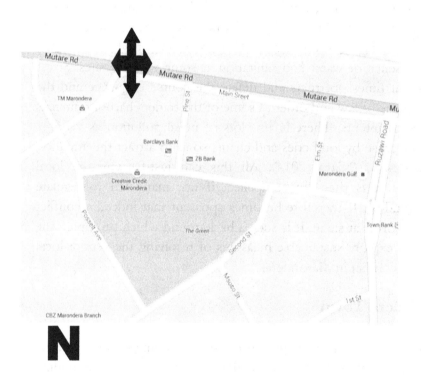

Source: Google Maps (Marondera CBD)

This is the area which has proved itself to be the "melting pot" in as far as the vendor-local authority impasse is concerned. Vendors

8

and the Municipality are the major conflicting parties in the stalemate and efforts to manage the conflict, resolve the conflict or to improve relations focused on these two camps. However, the book also renders attention to contributions and aspirations of the general public and the central government through the Ministry of Small to Medium Scale Enterprises.

CHAPTER 2

Taking Lessons from other Related Cases. Dealing with the vendor-local authority conflict

Harare Municipality, Zimbabwe

Whilst local authorities have made some efforts to address the vendor-local authority conflict, the limitations with their efforts has been that they have placed the management of such a crisis in the hands of wrong departments. More often than not, even with Harare Municipality, municipal traffic cops seem to be the ones who also deal with vendors. In this regard, vendors are viewed as a problem that has to be controlled rather than a production unit that contributes to the urban economy, (Mitullah, 2003).

It would actually be better to entrust the social services departments or revenue departments with the management of the vendor-local authority conflict because they will appreciate better the socio-economic and political background of street vending hence increase the chances of finding sustainable measures of resolving such conflicts.

Kumasi City, Ghana

Ayeh, Emefa, Sylvana and Isaac (2009) condemned what they termed the bulldozer approach which at times is adopted by Kumasi City Authorities as they attempt to destroy some vending structures. This can also be termed the fire-fighting approach, which only reacts after

10

a problem would have manifested itself and does little to address the root causes to the problem. Local authorities need to desist from such approaches as they seek to resolve the vendor-local authority crisis for such approaches do little in finding sustainable solutions. It has been proved that despite such drastic measures, vendors will always re-appear. Nevertheless, at least with Kumasi City authorities, prior to any decongestion exercise, a notice of eviction with a deadline of about two weeks is given and there are few sporadic raids (Ayeh, Emefa, Sylvana and Isaac, 2009).

In their study, Ayeh, et al (2009), did not find evictions of street traders as a sustainable measure of resolving a vendor-local authority conflict. In fact, one will tend to question the logic behind some forced evictions as at times they appear to be futile and costly. According to the MEC, one reason why decongestion exercises are not much of a success is a lack of logistics. The amount of money spent on security personnel and other members of the demolition team is high and so could not be maintained. A soon as the decongestion momentum goes down, vendors will still return to the streets. With this background, a shadow of doubt is cast on the sustainability of solely relying on raids and eviction as a way of dealing with the vendor crisis.

The role of the civic society in resolving the vendor-local authority conflict

There is a great possibility that the civic society can be very instrumental in addressing this conflict as history can confirm that the civic society once helped even in solving some political situations and civil wars. One may also consider the role played by the Church in bringing an end to the apartheid era, just to mention but a few.

Gutsa, Dodo, Mutsau, Hlatywayo, and Majoni (2011) specified that civic society is a term used to refer to non-state actors or stakeholders who take it upon themselves to specialize on various subjects which tend to affect the environment, human, plant and animal life, be it socially, economically, politically or otherwise. These come up in forms of lobby groups, advocacy groups, and religious institutions and so on. Some advocate for human rights, labour relations, citizen participation and so on. Generally they are known as Non-Governmental Organizations. In Marondera, one of those is known as Citizen Participation Trust. According to Gutsa et al. (2011), these groups can also play an important mediation role by facilitating effective and sustainable dialogue between at least two conflicting parties, in this case vendors and the municipality.

Cheema (2011:8) also made a similar observation when he found out that "in urban areas, civil society organizations have played a major role over the years in urban shelter, services and protecting the interests of slum dwellers and squatters in government initiated programs." This means that without an active civic society in Marondera, the vending community can be at the mercy of the local authority which will have the sole responsibility of determining the future and destiny of vendors. The municipality becomes the judge in a case to which it is also a conflicting party and under such circumstances, justice is not guaranteed.

Cheema (2011:8) also went on to propound that the civic society organizes poor urban communities to help them gain access to land titles and basic urban services such as water, sanitation, primary health care and education. This is a realization of the fact that the vending community, as earlier on alluded to, can be best described as a disadvantaged group if not a vulnerable one. They need help to get themselves organized and speak with one voice, especially when it comes to demanding their rights or legal recognition. On the other hand, pressure has to be mounted on the local authorities so that they execute their mandate of service delivery, something which some of them seem to be gradually neglecting despite collecting revenue.

Any meaningful conflict resolution process will require a mediator who is independent and impartial.

Iran

Mohammadi, Nrazizan and Shahvandi (2011) reiterated the mediation role which was played by the civic society in resolving vendor-local authority conflicts in Iran. In doing so, they further emphasized the significance of participation in this call hence they asserted that there is a trilateral relationship between people's participation in local government, civic engagement and good governance. These three facets are seen as the basic foundation for people's empowerment and it is only when these three facets are able to correlate well that meaningful peace within the jurisdiction of local governance can become a reality.

The role of urban planning in resolving the vendor-local authority conflict

The role of urban planning in dealing with this kind of conflicts should never be underestimated. It is unfortunate that some scholars, in addressing this subject make an oversight of the role urban planning can play in breaking the conflict or rather the role played by urban planning in causing the conflict.

Brown (2006) also explored the role which could be played by urban planning in resolving a vendor-local conflict. In doing so, she

13

took special cognizance of the importance of urban public space to the poor and this means that not inculcating the needs of the poor in urban planning will not do any good in resolving the impasse in question. Brown (2006) alluded that although urban public space is a common resource, it is not static, but a shifting resource whose boundaries may change quickly over time as a result of social negotiation. This means that changes can always be made taking into account the socio-economic and political dynamics of the society and it would not be fair for any municipality to remain rigid and refuse to make any alterations as may be deemed necessary. It is good that she found value in negotiation and its capability in finding an amicable solution amongst conflicting parties. In most cases, local authorities have given the impression that boundaries in the Central Business Districts are so fixed such that there is no longer any space to negotiate for, but it has since been proved not to be the case.

When resolving the vendor-local authority conflict, not only do vendors have to contribute in policy formulation, but they also have to add their voice in Urban Planning. This will help them appreciate why certain pieces of land have been allocated particular land uses, and for what reason. They will also negotiate mutual places for vending sites, (Roever, 2010).

One may actually wonder why vendors find themselves so much concentrated around the Central Business Districts. The answer is within a school of thought which subscribes to the view that markets operate best around commercial centers, public transport termini or other areas with high pedestrian flows. According to this school of thought, it means a bid to wipe off vendors from such prime areas might not only prove to be difficult, but may impact negatively economically and socially. There is therefore, a need for a paradigm shift in the way in which urban planners perceive vendors if ever vendor-local authority conflicts are to become a thing of the past, (Dewar and Watson, 1990). Walsh (2010:160) also lamented the fact that;

> Urban planners have tended to consider street vendors… as nuisances to be hidden out of sight or at least placed into idealized locales where they may be consumers as part of a culture of museums tourism but in situations which may not be convenient for drawing customers, especially when the principal competitive advantage that vendors offer customers are convenient through location.

This view takes the resolving of vendor-local authority conflict beyond vendors or city fathers but also to physical urban planners as well. They need to change their view and come up with urban planning which sees a reasonable sharing of the urban prime land, (Roever, 2010).

The City of Dar es Salaam, Tanzania

The City of Dar es Salaam in Tanzania is one other typical example whereby city vendors have been accommodated. Skinner (2008) reported that as early as in the 1990's street vendors in Dar es Salaam were issued with licenses and allowed to trade. Therefore, its high time vendors be accommodated than to be viewed as enemies.

Vending machines

Some other countries, particularly in the Americas have made a successful use of the so called vending machines. Vending machines are automated and offer a self-service opportunity to clients on a wide range variety of commodities. Vending machines dispenses food, drinks, chewing gums, toiletries or any other type of merchandise when money is inserted. Modern vending machines can accept coins and paper money, and some accept pre-paid tokens. Some pre-paid vending machines require that the exact amount of money for a particular item be inserted, but an increasing number of vending machines can make change, (Microsoft Encarta Premium 2009).

Vending machines have in the Americas been used for various reasons. It is on this basis that probably the Municipality of Marondera may consider exploring the possibility of introducing vending machines so as to decongest the town of vendors. This however, is likely to evoke some mixed reactions particularly among the vending community as they are likely to be driven out of business and the possibility of a win-win peaceful situation may become a far-fetched assumption. On the other hand, the generality of the public would likely welcome such an orderly concept.

San Diego, USA

The County of San Diego adopted a Healthy Vending Machine Policy for health reasons and also as a way of regulating the type and standard of food that find its way on to the market, (*The Health Vending Machine Policy of the County of San Diego Department of Parks and Recreation*). On March 23, 2006, the Country of San Diego Department of Parks and Recreation adopted a health vending machine Policy. The policy required that food and beverages sold in vending machines located in all facilities under the jurisdictions of the department meet specified nutritious standards.

This was seen as a measure which could see a reduction in child obesity, something which had become a cause for concern in San Diego at the time the policy was adopted. Mealey (2009), however, questioned the sanity of such vending machines. He alleged that, instead, they are actually a source of less than healthy products thus adding more confusion to the whole debate. In other words, vending machines can also come along with several health implications, both positive and negative, but of importance is to highlight that they need not be ruled out but rather, their impact in solving the conflict at hand may need to be explored.

Formalizing vending

The other reason to blame for the vendor-local authority conflict is a lack of proper recognition of the vending community. Mitullah (2003) argues that street trade has in the past been viewed as an underground activity that instead undermines the healthy function of the formal economy. The accuracy of this statement can however be questioned, especially when taking into account the fact that it has actually been established that the informal economy, vendors included, actually support the formal economy in that they purchase their commodities for resale and they also hire transport and other related costs from the formal economy. Therefore, undermining or not recognizing vendors may not only be unjust but also be unfair.

In actual fact, in Zimbabwe, there is no longer much formal sector to talk about especially when considering that the economy is in a recession phase. Families have actually been sustained through these informal business ventures, chief amongst them, vending.

Thailand, Cambodia, Mongolia and Nigeria

Illegalizing vending is tantamount to acriminalization of vending so as to speak. According to Kusakabe (2006), street vending in Thailand, Cambodia and Mongolia is viewed as illegal. This has been through some laws such as *Cleanliness and Order of the City Act of 1992*, the *Traffic and Land Transportation Act of 1992* and *the Highway Act of 1993*. The net effect of all this has been a lack of social security on vending enterprises. No business bank accounts, no pension, no medical aids and no formal policies and this in other words facilitates a perpetuation of poverty, (Kusakabe, 2006). Certainly, this calls for the legal status of vendors to be improved as a way of resolving the vendor-local authority conflict. Anetor (2015) generally found out that in Nigeria, there are just no clear cut laws guiding street vending and licenses are very hard to get.

Broomley (2000) also bemoaned the fact that national governments just do not take the issue of vending seriously such that it is rarely on the government's list of priorities or even on national budgets despite the potential of such a sector to contribute positively to the Gross Domestic Product. In order to resolve the vendor-local authority conflict, governments now need to take vending seriously, re-capitalizing vending by making some budget allocations to it and this will make vending a viable business venture and local authorities will also be set to benefit out of it.

Asia

In Asia, it is also not all that rosy for street vendors. Njaya (2014) reported that in almost all the Asian Countries, street vendors do not have a legal status and they are constantly harassed by authorities, (Bhowmik, 2005 in Njaya, 2014). This further adds weight to the calls of formalization of street vending so that it can also be recognized as a legal economic sector. That way, the vendor-local authority conflict would have been half-solved.

Vendor Statistics

Without a consideration of statistics, there is no serious planning. That is the reason why at national levels governments conduct censuses to establish population size, gender ratios, statuses and so on so that they can effectively plan and come up with meaningful policy formulation that is tailor-made for particular areas. However, this is not the case with local authorities particularly in Kenya, Cote D'Ivor, Ghana, Zimbabwe, Uganda and South Africa, as established by Mitullah (2005).

He noted that even local authorities who collect substantial revenue from the sector do not maintain records of the contribution of the sector to urban economy. This calls for an urgent need in most local authorities to conduct research studies similar to this one and establish the extent to which vending has contributed to the livelihood of human kind in Africa before resisting its initiatives.

However, Roever (2010) makes a candid observation to the effect that the population sizes of street vendors in any given locality is exceedingly difficult to measure. This is so especially when taking into account the fact that a good number of them are not licensed, hence not in municipalities' data bases. Their mobile nature further compounds the situation. Now, as indicated earlier on, when statistics are not clear or known, no effective and relevant urban planning will take place. Roever (2010) also went on to bemoan the fact that most existing estimates undercount the total numbers of people working in the streets. Such misrepresentation is misleading and at most offers a serious disadvantage to vendors.

Citizen participation in local governance

There has been a plethora of studies confirming the fact that citizen participation and local governance should never be separated under normal circumstances. Various scholars have given a more or less the same definitions of (civic) participation. Initially, Dodo and Mateura (2011: 36) gave an elementary definition of participation to the effect that it is to contribute, to chip in, to join, to involve and to take part. Probably after having realized that they had only given a mere dictionary meaning, they went a step further to define participation in some more technical terms; "participation in social sciences refers to different mechanisms for the public to express opinions regarding political, economic, management and other social decisions", (Dodo and Mateura, 2011:50).

Such a definition inevitably takes one to a consideration of the International Covenant on Economic, Social and Cultural Rights of 1960, which is one other component of the United Nations Human Rights Charter to which Zimbabwe is a signatory. Dodo and Mateura (2011:51) also went further to quote Amstein (1969) who gave a more politically inclined definition of participation; "citizen participation is the redistribution of power that enables the have-not citizens, presently excluded from the political and economic processes to be deliberately included in the future". This is more or less the same with Klein's (2005:1) view that the right to political participation refers to citizens' right to seek to influence public affairs. Public affairs might include the activities of residents, vendors, civic associations, neighborhood groups, social movements, social clubs as well as formal procedures of government.

It is therefore apparent from the above cited definitions that citizen participation is not only of significant importance when it comes to local governance but is actually very instrumental when it comes to the exploration of sustainable measures of resolving the vendor-local authority conflict particularly in Marondera. It brings different stakeholders together and it is highly likely that decisions will be arrived at by a general consensus and this may minimize conflicts. Goventa and Valderama (1999) added weight to the debate by alluding the fact that the concept of participation is being related to rights of citizenship and democratic governance. This means that a failure to incorporate the vending community who are part of the citizenry in the policy formulation or review even at municipal level is very much undemocratic and where democracy does not prevail violence is not a remote possibility.

It should however, be noted that this challenge of vending or rather the vendor-local authority conflict is not something peculiar to Marondera Municipality but rather it is a challenge which has been seen the world over with the Latin America being a typical example. It is also important for one to realize that in a bid to resolve an existing kind of conflict, citizen participation comes in various forms and the local authority will have to explore any of the forms or some of the forms of civil participation if not all the forms of civic participation since it is greatly anticipated that chances are very high that positive peace will be achieved.

The other types of participation include: 1. physical participation - being present, using one's skills and effects; 2. mental participation - conceptualizing the active, decision making, organization and management; 3. emotional participation - assuming responsibility,

21

power authority; 4. manipulative participative - participation in pretense with people's representatives on official boards but who are unelected and have no power;participation for material incentives – people participate by contributing resources, e.g. labour in return for material incentives; 5. participation by consultation – people participate by being consulted or by answering questions, external agents define problems and information gathering process and so control analysis; 6. (Adopted from Zanna, 2015:19, Meldon, Walsh and Kenny, 2000:1) set mobilization participation – people participate by taking initiative, they develop contacts with external bodies for resources and technical advice that they need, but in return control over how the resources are used; 7. interactive participation – people participate in joint analysis, development of action plans and the formation of strengthening of local institutions andparticipation can be top-down or bottom-up – uniform or diverse, simple or complex, static or dynamic, controllable or uncontrollable, predictable or unpredictable, (Adopted from Zanna, 2015:19, Meldon, Walsh and Kenny, 2000:1).

One other advantage of citizen participation as a tool of solving disputes is that it gives agency to the voiceless and the marginalized. A failure to do this can be best described in Galtung's terms as a latent conflict which in simple words is a time bomb which can actually one way or the other prove to be fatal. In this regard, the same policy brief actually made a plausible observation to the effect that;

> In fact by allowing greater participation or groups that were historically left out of decision making process, such as women, youths and indigenous populations, these local councils (Latin

America) have made local governance more inclusive and representative.

It is actually a fact that even in the Central Business District of Marondera the youths and women form the majority of vending community yet when it comes to decision making such groups are the least represented. This will not do any good in trying to resolve the impasse in question. Zanna (2015:18) also chips in, but from another different angle. Zanna believes that citizen participations breeds a sense of belonging amongst the population and of the population, the vending community included does have a sense of belonging, they are less likely to rebel against existing rules and regulations but rather they become vanguards of the same and thus they become their own police. However, he did not have kind words for local authorities as he urged them to design people-oriented development programs. This would mean that an attempt to flush out vendors form the Central Business District may not yield any positive results.

It is also his firm belief that in a bid to promote peace, participation is a basic ingredient and a component of good governance. This will mean providing an inclusive and popular participation in government that which respects the rule of law, transparency, accountability prevention of corruption, effectiveness and efficient public management systems and processes. Good governance provides a response and center-oriented governance to the people and this ensures legitimate governance and democratic instructions, (Zanna 2015: 20).

Complying with by-laws

The disadvantages of vending are what necessitates the existence of by-laws in a bid to try and regulate vending at the same time eliminating its negative effects. Anetor (2015) found out that street vending is one other good source of outbreaks of diseases. He further argued that street vending poses many dangers particularly to the girl child, who is a common feature in street vending through forfeiting her education.

The conflict between vendors and local authorities cannot be wholly blamed on municipalities, but also on vendors themselves. Willemse (2009) actually came to the conclusion that high levels of competition between vendors negatively affects their operations. You find a whole lot mass of people selling same goods, products and food stuffs, at the same place and at the same time. This significantly lowers the prices and quality much to the disadvantage of vendors. Vendors need to know basic marketing and business skills so that inter-group conflicts are minimized if not eradicated at all.

According to Smith (2009) there was a general acknowledgement of the fact that;

> Local citizen participation has long been acknowledged as a useful tool to enhance public policies: it improves policies' responsiveness to the population's needs and quality as citizens make creative and innovative proposals to solve development challenges.

The impression given here is that engaging the community and in this case the vendors, should not be a matter of choice or privilege, but rather a must if by any means vendors are to cooperate and comply with regulations. This is because they would have somehow taken part and contributed in proposing ways of solving developmental challenges and that way the adverse effects of the vendor-local authority conflict can be minimized.

The current state of affairs in most local authorities, Marondera included is that it would appear as if it is now practically impossible for the local authority to collect the much needed revenue in form of fees and taxes from vendors.

Khumasi, Ghana

Ayeh, Emefa, Sylvana and Isaac (2009) gave a typical case study of street vending and the use of public space in Kumasi, Ghana, where they actually established that the majority of vendors were indeed paying taxes and Marondera Municipality can also look forward toward the same.

In their study, they found out that 75% of vendors paid some fees daily or monthly while a paltry 25% did not. Different authorities received the fees paid. About 93% is paid directly to a Kumasi Municipality Officer whilst in a few cases of about 1% of the fees is paid to shop owners whose frontage the street vendors operate on. This demonstrates that as a way of regulating volumes of vendors who operate on other people's shop fronts, such shop owners can put in place a fee for that. Income tax to the Internal Revenue Services constituted 3.6% while 2.3% paid fees to the chairpersons of various street vendors associations. This further shows how vendors in Kumasi are a bit organized and how they take seriously the issue of their own associations, (Ayeh, Emefa, Sylvana and Isaac, 2009).

EThekwini Municipality, South Africa: Informal Trading By-Law, 2014:

To provide for the right to engage in informal trading areas and informal trading sites on municipal property; to provide for the granting of trading permits to trade on municipal property; to restrict and prohibit informal trading in certain areas; to regulate the conduct of informal traders; to regulate informal trading at special events; to provide for measures to ensure health and safety; to create offences and penalties; to provide for the repeal of laws and savings; and to provide for matters incidental thereto.

Nevertheless, there is need to peacefully strike a balance between the interests of justice, the interests of the municipality, interests of vendors and interests of the general population. The fact that the eThekwini Municipal By-Laws were passed in 2014 also further exposes the Municipality of Marondera By-Laws of 1986 as far much outdated and not in tandem with modern dynamic trends.

Mitullah (2003) categorically stated that local authorities in Africa are one major obstacles to the development of informal sector activities through outdated restrictive by-laws most of which were enacted during the colonial era. What this means is that to rectify such a challenge, local authorities become an instrumental stakeholder and reforms of the local authorities, as proposed by Meldon, Walsh and Kenny (2000) may be inevitable so as to enhance good local governance and citizen participation for the benefit of all.

Colonial legacy in African cities by-laws

An impression has been given that in most African cities, the existing by-laws are a perpetuation of a colonial legacy which was designed in such a way so as to minimize or completely outlaw black majority business activities such as vending from Central Business District.

However, a look at the City of Cambridge by-laws (2009) may prove otherwise. Below are some of the relevant extracts. The Corporation of the City of Cambridge (Britain). Outdoor Vendors By-law # 106-09 (2009)

6. Any person, licensed pursuant to the provision of this by law shall;

(b) Not operate within 5 meters of an intersection

(c) Not operate… on a public side walk

(d) Not operate within 30 meters of the nearest corner of the competing commercial establishment

(e) Not operate within one hundred meters of any elementary or secondary school   property

(f) Not operate within 30 meters of any other outdoor vendor

The above cited by-laws would actually indicate that they are actually more repressive than the ones we have here in Africa. For example, Section 6 (b) (c) (d) (e) (f) indicate that vending is not allowed some meters away from shops, intersections and schools. This would only permit very few isolated vendors to operate. In African Cities vending By-Laws, there are very few if any such repressive laws. The gist of this input is to the effect that to try and explain by-laws on colonial grounds maybe misplaced as the ones we had even during the colonial time are quite flexible compared to the ones which even Europe has today. However, it should be noted that vending in the European context appears not to be the same in the African context. Vendors in this context vary in numbers, frequency and types of goods sold. A look at the Cambridge by-laws will indicate that their vending mainly focuses on stuff such as ice-creams, hot dogs and beverages yet ours goes beyond that to include perishables, clothing, electrical and other second hand goods. Ours is fueled by unemployment and a search for survival which may not be the case in Europe hence drawing comparison between the two should be done cautiously.

Vending policies which establishes a win-win situation

There is no doubt that the whole essence of any conflict resolution process should be to establish a win-win situation. As conceded by Njaya (2014), there is no doubt Zimbabwe is yet to come up with a framework of street vending governing and regulating vending in all Zimbabwean cities. This book also sought to close such a gap. Nevertheless, it would appear that a good number of the Americas and European countries have made strides in coming up with national vending policies. Such countries include the United States of America, the United Kingdom, France, India, Peru, Barbados and the Bahamas. Zimbabwe needs to quickly join the league. Certainly without a clear policy, conflicts between vendors and local authorities are likely to escalate, (Njaya, 2014).

Of late, local authorities have been coming up with by-laws, regulations and policies without even consulting the people concerned and affected by the same. As a democratic process, there is a need to consult widely and seek the contribution of masses in the formulation of policies, and that way, chances of complying with such measures put in place will be very high.

Vietnam

In Vietnam, some laws were passed, legislation which confers upon citizens the rights to be informed of government activities that affect them, to discuss and contribute to the formulation of certain plans and projects, to participate in local development and to supervise government performance. This has been through laws such as *Democracy Strengthening at Local Level Decree, Decree 29/1998/ND-CP of May 11, 1998* which was then succeeded by the *Grassroots Democracy Decree, Decree 79, 2003* before being upgraded to an ordinance in 2007. All this shows how some governments have taken seriously the issue of citizen participation and this is very much instrumental when it comes to solving a vendor-local authority conflict.

The concept of a world class city

Whilst it is very much welcome that most African local authorities (municipalities) are talking of the desire of reaching a "world class city" status, say by (vision) 2020, it is also this same desire that can also be blamed for sour relations between vendors and local authorities, (Jongh, 2015). They desire their cities and towns such as Harare and Marondera to reach levels such as those of New York City, Paris and London where according to Jongh (2015) contemporary planning practices in the global south do not accept informality. The question which one may ask is how applicable is such a stance in African cities and towns. The socio-economic and political situations and background of America and Europe differ from that of Africa whereby poverty, economic under-performance and unemployment normally reach alarming levels. This therefore questions the logic of African local authorities not allowing vending to take place in areas under their jurisdiction whilst dreaming of attaining a "world class city" status within a short space of time.

Vending associations

In addressing a vendor-local authority conflict, vendor-associations become of paramount importance. It is however sad that in most African cities, it is either there are no vendor associations or the few available are just ineffective. According to Mitullah (2003), the associations are poorly organized, they have no bargaining power and cannot effectively advocate for vendors rights to trade and to contribute to the urban economy. Most of the associations seem to focus more on welfare issues with very few focusing on business issues such as service provision, site operation, licensing and policy issues (Mitullah, 2003; Brown, Potoski and Slyke, 2007).

However, Mitullah (2003) singled out South Africa as having better organized vending organizations which actually offer business services to members such as bulk-purchase, storage, marketing, training, negotiation and advocacy. The existence, if any, of such associations in Marondera was explored. Mitullah (2003) further lamented the fact that the problem with most vending associations is that they are issue driven. They appear and disappear, depending on a felt need.

As a way of resolving the vendor-local authority conflict and also as a way of effectively empowering vendors much to the benefit of all, Njaya (2014) recommended that vending associations need to be established. This will help in putting up resources together for a much bigger investment in say, real estate which can then be developed and rented to members and other informal traders. This means it is now high time vendors should be owning shopping malls and other properties. If this is implemented, vending will never be the same in Marondera and Zimbabwe at large.

Latin America

As has been the case in most parts of the world, only a small fraction of street vendors in Latin America have access to any kind of state sponsored social protection schemes. For example, less than 20% of street vendors in Lima, Peru are enrolled in a pension scheme and are affiliated with a health care system. This therefore calls for governments and local authorities together with vendors to try and come up with means of how they may organize social security schemes which in a way will benefit vendors in terms of life cover and at the same time benefit local governance in terms of revenue and thus establishing a win-win situation. That is according to Roever (2010).

India

Actually, very few street vending associations such as the *Self Employed Women's Association of India* have managed to sustain group insurance. A lot still needs to be done in the organization of such associations.

The Informal Economy Monitoring Study conducted a research in Ahmedabad, India, whereupon 152 food and non-food street vendors were surveyed with about 75 people also taking part in some focus group discussions. Amongst others, the following were noted to be some of the advantages which come along with street vending.

Street vending is a source of living for many households; **1.** street vending provides a refuge to those retrenched; **2.** vendors provide affordable goods and fresh produce in convenient locations; **3.** informal vendors' enterprises are linked to formal economic enterprises in the sense that it was found out that about 83% of vendors acquire goods they sell from formal enterprises; **4.** through their transport needs, vendors create employment for head loaders, porters and auto rickshaw drivers; **5.** some food vendors contribute revenue to the city through tax paid at wholesale markets. (The same is true with Dombotombo farm produce market in Marondera) and 72% of vendors responded to lower revenue by borrowing from money lenders creating a cycle of taking and repaying small loans.

It is however disturbing that as has always been the norm in the developing world, many street vendors in Ahmedabad are being displaced by urban infrastructure and development projects. Fortunately, there has been some positive intervention with some members of the civic society offering legal aid and support against evictions, harassments and confiscation of their goods. Furthermore, the Gujarat Unorganized Labor Welfare Board was felt to have had a positive impact for providing identity cards, tools required for their trade, education scholarships for children, skills upgrading, amongst others and thus also further showing the important role that which can be played by the civic society in such a discourse.

Kenya

In Kenya, it was found out that vending falls within the Small to Medium Scale Entrepreneurship category, that which provides employment and income to about 70% of Kenya's population, especially in the urban areas. Therefore, such a role of street vending cannot be undermined. In this context, formalization of street vending comes along with it some benefits, chief amongst them property rights, reduced barriers to market entry and an introduction of cost effective regulations and democratic policy processes, (Mitullah, 2003 and Njaya, 2014).

Credit lines for vendors

The hope is, if vendors are well financed, it is most likely that they will get organized, they we will be able to comply with by-laws, particularly paying up license fees and they would also be able to meet basic health standard. It is however common cause that such is not the case with most urban vendors. They are under-funded.

It is unfortunate that financing or re-capitalization of vendors has never been taken seriously by most local authorities. Mitullah (2003) reported that in most cases financing is non-existent at all, and if ever it becomes available, the interest rates are so high and at around 20%. In light of the above situation, the main source of finance for vendors has been rotating Savings Credit Associations locally known in Marondera as *maroundi* or *mikando*.

The disadvantage of such a form of financing has been that it provides low amounts of finance that are not adequate for expanding the trade in an organized and law compliant manner. Furthermore, the associations are plagued by governance problems, including leadership and mismanagement. This also calls for efforts to find means of how vending can be effectively funded and how their associations can also be effective.

As a solution to the above challenge, Mitullah (2003) realized that in countries such as Kenya, street traders suggested the establishment of Micro-Entrepreneurs Bank that can avail loans to small and medium scale entrepreneurship at reasonable rates. In this cited case, the traders were of the opinion that such an establishment would operate better if placed under the umbrella of a government ministry.

Kumasi, Ghana

In Kumasi, according to Ayeh, Emefa, Sylvana and Isaac (2009), street vendors work with soft loans which are payable back within three months. Vendors are also able to purchase perishable goods for resale on credit then pay later at the end of the day with some interest after realizing some profits. This reflects the importance of supporting vending initiatives with some credit lines so that they become established thereby sustaining the formal economy and lessen up conflicts. Ayeh, Emefa, Sylvana and Isaac (2009), actually found out that in Kumasi, the displacement of vendors through evictions has thus interrupted with their income flows through destabilization and whenever this is done, it impacts negatively when it comes to servicing of their credit facilities and loans, hence evictions at times serve no good purpose at all and it is a threat to efforts of establishing a win-win situation.

Arusha, Tanzania

In Arusha, local government officials no longer perform arbitrary evictions but rather they support the informal sector with some loans. According to David et al. (2009), the case study also demonstrates that improving the city environment is possible without necessarily disrupting livelihoods in the informal economy, opting instead to improve its performance by leveraging it with local formal enterprises.

Delegating the management of markets to informal traders, as a way of resolving the vendor-local authority conflict

One way to establish a win-win situation is whereby local authorities give the management of certain vending sites or markets to vendors themselves. They will become their own police, hence grooming a sense of responsibility and there will be increased tax collections on the part of local authorities.

Bamako, Mali

According to David, Ulrich, Zelzeck and Majoe (2009) the implementation of the delegated management of vending markets approach in Bamako, Mali led to an increased revenue collection. Their working environment was improved. David et al (2009) thus stressed that in countries such as Mali, where the whole economy is virtually informal, such types of partnerships can be catalysts for real development of the national economy because they directly contribute to the improvement of the informal economy productivity through a greater consideration of the challenges faced by the sector and thus such an approach would alleviate the adverse effects of the vendor-local authority conflict.

CHAPTER 3:

THEORETICAL FRAME WORK UNDERPINNING THE VENDOR-LOCAL AUTHORITY CONFLICT

Basically, this book is deeply grounded and rooted in the Community Relations Theory and the Paul John Lederech's pyramid model.

The Community Relations Theory

The architects of this theory assumed that conflict is caused by an on-going polarization, mistrust and hostility between different groups within a community. The goals of work based on community relations theory are; 1. to improve communication and understanding between conflicting groups and, 2. to promote greater tolerance and acceptance of diversity in the community (Fisher et al., 2000:8).

It cannot be doubted that the conflict between vendors and the local authority can be best described as a polarized one. They are two worlds apart and none amongst the conflicting parties seem to be taking each other's concerns seriously. This partly explains the running battles on regular intervals between vendors and municipal police. Therefore, on the bedrock of the community relations theory, this book sought to improve communication and understanding between the conflicting parties.

According to Otite (2001), conflict resolution carries out a healing function amongst various groups in a society. It was further argued that this occurs by providing the opportunity for parties involved to examine alternative pay-off in a conflict situation. It also places the conflicting parties, and in this case the vendors and the local authority, in a situation in which they can choose alternative positive means for resolving their differences. Otite, as quoted by Amodu also explained that consensus building, social bridge reconstructions, and the reenactment of order in the society are achieved through conflict resolution. Basically, that is also how the community relations theory can be seen to be the bed rock of this book as well as explained from various angles.

Unfortunately, this theory only fell short in that it then did not outline how its goals can be achieved. It would appear the presumption was that conflicts are simple yet in actual fact they can be very complicated and protracted. Furthermore, this theory does not clearly outline the probable conflict parties to such a conflict and this is a gap which got closed by the John Paul Lederech's Pyramid Model. (Fisher et al., 2000:8).

John Paul Lederech's Pyramid Model

The significance of this model, as outlined by Fisher et al (2000:33) is that it is a graphic tool showing some stakeholders who may be available, affected, involved, causing or who can help alleviate a conflict. This is of much importance when it comes to the aspect of conflict analysis and conflict mapping.

The illustration below shows the pyramid/three level triangle

level 1

le vlv 1ry/polvtic1l le1der1

lw erv1tiov1l orv1vvltiov1

lvoverve ev oe cvll1

level 1

lre1pec ed 1ec orvl le1der1

le dvvc/relwvoc 1 le1der1

l1c1dee vc1

le v d 1 le1der1

lprofe11vov1l1

level 1

lloc1l le1der1/elder1

le v d 1 1vd coe e cvvy worker1

lwoe ev 1vd yoc d vroc p1

lloc1l de1l d oe cvll1

lrefcvee c1e p le1der1

l1ctivvl 1

Source: (Fisher et al., 2000; 33).

Some purposes of the above pyramid include; 1. to identify key actors including leadership at each level; 2. to assess what types of approaches or actions are appropriate; 3. to consider ways to build links between levels andplanning actions to address a multi-level conflict (Fisher et al., 2000; 33).

The pyramid/triangle gives an almost true reflection of each and every society. The few elite members are found at the top of the pyramid and also happen to be the least affected by any calamity that may befall the community, whilst it is the ordinary men, vendors included who are found at the base of the pyramid. These are many in numbers and they are the ones who bear the brunt. Usually, and under a "gravitational pull" any ideas or policies would cascade from the top going downwards but a sustainable strategy will be that which will incorporate the masses at the base especially during policy formulation stage. That is citizenry participation. Each level of the pyramid can be categorized as; the elite, the middle level and lower level. All these factors need to be holistically considered as sustainable measures of managing the vendor-local authority conflict are explored.

At the top levels of the pyramid, we can say there is the local authority (the municipality). There is no doubt that this group is sustained by the general populace, which is found at the base of the pyramid, and this includes vendors. In terms of numbers, the latter group is much bigger. Any conflict between the two groups need to be amicably resolved for a peaceful and sustainable coexistence. Thus the middle level of the pyramid does comprise of the civic society, the academia, the religious can as well have a meaningful role in the resolving of the vender-local authority conflict as spelt out by the pyramid model.

In essence, the cited theories offer a reinforcement to the core foundations of this book,(Fisher et al., 2000).

CHAPTER 4:

THE CASE OF MARONDERA MUNICIPALITY

An Analysis of the Marondera (Hawkers and Street Vendors) By-Laws, 1986. CAP 134

The book; *A Cat & Mouse Affair, Exploring Sustainable Measures of Resolving the Vendor-Local Authority Conflict: A Case of Marondera Municipality, Zimbabwe* would be incomplete or baseless if it is to be finalized without a scrutiny of Marondera Municipality's vending by-laws. Basically, these are rules and regulations which govern and regulate vending in the town hence they are of primary importance. The author finds it very essential to replicate some few relevant sections of the by-laws as they are before an analysis of them is done.Marondera (Hawkers and Street Vendors) By-Laws, 1986. CAP 134

Authority of trade

3. No person shall carry on the business of a hawker or street vendor unless he has been issued with a registration certificate by the council.

Refusal of Application for, or renewal of, registration certificates

7. The council may, in its discretion, refuse to issue, renew or vary a registration certificate if

In the opinion of the council such issue, renewal or variation would adversely affect existing trade or business in the area under its jurisdiction or

In the opinion of the council, such issue, renewal or variation is not in the interest of public health or safety or

The applicant has been convicted of

Any offence under these by-laws or

Any offence under the trade measures Act Chapter 298

Any offence under the public Health Act (Chapter 167) or

Any offence involving dishonesty, and has been sentenced to imprisonment without the option of a fine; or

In the opinion of the council, such issue, renewal or variation would result in overtrading of goods listed in the application.

Cancellation of Registration Certificates

8. (1) the council may cancel any registration certificate of the holder thereof, at any time after the issue of such registration certificate if

(a) Has been convicted of any offence set out in paragraph (c) of section 7

(2) The council shall cancel any registration certificate if the holder is dealing in food and is found to be suffering from a communicable disease.

Identification of Hawkers/street vendors

9 (i) … a badge bearing the year and number of registration certificate, with the inscription "Registered hawker/street vendor".

Hours of business

17. No person shall carry on the business of a hawker or street vendor between hours of 6pm and 8 am.

Repeal

18.   The Marondera (Hawker) By-Laws, 1976, published in Rhodesia Government Notice 930 of 1976, are repealed.

In other words, section 3 of the by-laws (Authority to Trade) basically outlaws trading as a vendor without being licensed. Again this is two pronged. This is a mechanism or an instrument which ensures that the local authority will be able to regulate all traders for the benefit of the populace or for the benefit of the municipality one way or the other. On the other hand, trying to register each and every trader in the Central Business District may be unnecessarily restrictive and unnecessarily criminalizes many people.

Section 7 of the by-laws, Refusal of Application for, or Renewal of, Registration Certificate appears to have given the Municipality of Marondera an unfair advantage over vendors in the sense that it has once again become a judge in its own case in which it is also a conflicting part, an interested party, hence a conflict of interest is at stake. It is further disheartening to learn that section 7(c) and section 8 of the bylaws empowers the local authority not to issue licenses to ex-convicts of various offences and to cancel licenses to such persons. That is an obsolete retributive justice system which does no good to anyone. If such persons of such background are not allowed to trade, they are left which no other option, except to engage in crime and prostitution, something which the local authority or rather law enforcement agents seem to be struggling to also deal with.

Nowadays, there is a call for a restorative justice system, that which seeks to reform and re-engage ex-convicts for their benefit and for the benefit of the community. Maybe suspending issuance of licenses for a certain period to such persons would be a better option in the circumstances. This could be one other reason why most vendors have circumvented the process of applying for licenses and

43

chose to operate illegally thereby contributing to the conflict existing between the two parties.

Section 9(i) of the same talks about identification of hawkers/street vendors. It directs that any hawker should always put on a badge bearing the year and number of registration certificate with an inscription "registered hawker/street vendor" when operating. Upon conducting a general survey, the author could not even find a single street trader putting on such and one will be left to speculate if this means that few or none street traders have at all been registered, or rather it is a case of non-compliance, on the part of the traders. Thus, this book also endeavored to get to the bottom of the matter.

Section 17, hours of business, clearly outlaws any street vending during the night. Considering that this now appears to be the prime time when business is rife, as many people would be leaving their work places going back home and would require to carry home food, goodies and some commodities of some sort, the local authorities may need to revisit this clause and also try to explore how the municipality may also benefit from such a situation.

Section (18), (Repeal) will reveal that the current by-laws replaced those enacted a decade earlier in 1976 during the colonial era. Although the current by-laws then became effective in 1986 when Zimbabwe had already attained its independence, allegations to the effect that they are just a perpetuation of the colonial legacy as explained earlier on or a colonial hangover cannot be far-fetched.

However, one, or rather the local authority may be forgiven for denying such allegations which seem to portray that the sole intention of by-laws is to make life difficult for the people, but rather local authorities do come up with the by-laws for the good of the people. This becomes very much apparent especially as one tries to strike a comparison between Marondera municipality by-laws and those of other local authorities, even outside the country.

The author realised that if ever the Municipality of Marondera may contemplate coming up with an effective vending policy, then some demographic data has to be taken into consideration. From questionnaires distributed amongst the sample population, it turned out that the gender ratio of vendors operating within Marondera's Central Business District was more or less the same equal to each other as depicted below;

Demographic data

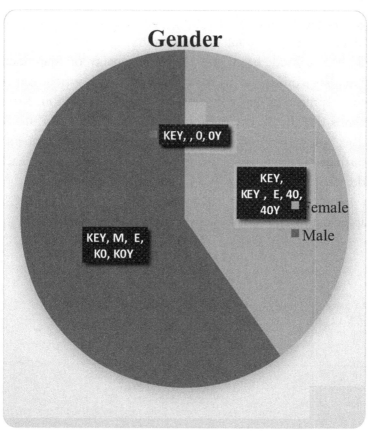

The gender ratio of vendors within Marondera's Central Business District

That may also mean that any conflict resolution process should thus take into account gender ratios and that there should be proportional representation of all in whatever sustainable dialogue which may take place.

Also in a bid to search for sustainable measures of resolving the vendor-local authority conflict in Marondera, age ranges were also found to be of paramount importance, especially in a bid to find which age groups were economically active and which were not and the reasons behind all that. Such data is vital when determining the feasibility of any mechanism that can be explored in a bid to resolve the vendor-local authority conflict. Below are the findings in that regard.

The percentages of various age groups who operate in Marondera's Central Business District

Age Group	Average %
18 years and below	5%
19-39 years	85%
40-49 years	5%
50 years and above	5%

Table 1

The questionnaire also sought to establish the exact status quo by way of seeking to understand the levels of education for the vending community in question. This may prove very useful for the policy maker when attempting to resolve the vendor-local authority conflict so that he or she knows the kind of people he or she is dealing with and their different levels of understanding. Whatever measures to be implemented have to be bear in mind the different educational levels of vendors in Marondera's Central Business District and the implications thereof. It emerged that the majority of vendors in Marondera went as far as Ordinary Level, education-wise and this also explains why Zimbabwe is considered to be a highly literate country.

Educational Levels %

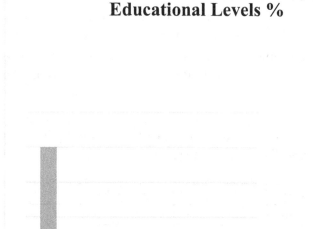

(Fig 4) levels of education of vendors in Marondera's CBD

The sustainability of any measure to be implored also has to take into consideration the average monthly incomes of vendors operating in Marondera's Central Business District. Through the questionnaire, the author managed to have a rough picture of the monthly incomes of vendors in question. It was unfortunate to learn that the majority of vendors realise a paltry amount of about $100 profit per month as profit.

Percentages of the vending sample and their average monthly income

Monthly income range	Percentage of vendors
Below $100	$60
$100-$250	$30
$250-$500	$10

Table 2

From the participants' choice of answers in the questionnaire, it became apparent that the majority of vendors operating in Marondera's Central Business District (about 90% of them) had vending as their only source of income. Furthermore, about 80% of the vending population in question indicated that they were the sole bread winners of their families with each family having an average of at least 3 dependents with some families having as high as 6 or more dependants. Largely, such a situation is due to the unavailability of jobs in the formal sector.

In trying to find some sustainable measures of alleviating the vendor-local authority conflict in Marondera, the author also sought to appreciate if the said vendors had some form of social security upon them. Below were the findings.

Table 3 Forms of social security and percentages of vendors in Marondera's CBD who are subscribed to them

Form of social security	% of vendors subscribed
pension	5%
Medical aid	5%

Funeral policy	10%
Educational policy	0%
None of the above	80%

In addition to that, the participants gave various reasons as to why they were not subscribed to the above cited forms of social security. Below are some of the common reasons which most of them gave for not being secured socially;

Because I don't have much money.
Business has not been all that good.
I left employment before the dollarization era.
I cannot afford all that since I survive on a hand to mouth basis.
I do not have a fixed salary.

It was also quite interesting to discover through the questionnaires that the majority of the vendors under study do not have a bank account and this can mean a lot in as far as business management is concerned. Only 30% of the participants indicated that they had bank accounts. The exorbitant bank charges actually make it difficult for someone not formally employed to maintain a bank account.

The author further had a focused group discussion with about 20 vendors as he also sought to find sustainable measures of resolving the vendor local-authority conflict in Marondera.

Sub-problem 1:

How can the conflict between vendors and the local authority be resolved peacefully and amicably?

From a discussion held, vendors complained that more often than not, they were always being displaced and chased away from the Central Business District by the Municipal Police. In fact, the majority of them concurred with each other that such raids do take place nearly on an hourly basis. Asked what reason they thought the Municipal Police chased them away from the Central Business District, almost all of them were fully aware that the reason was, that they operate at undesignated points and a few indicated that they were not licensed and at the same time not registered with the Municipality of Marondera. A question was then posed to them;

Q. *what do you expect the Municipality of Marondera to do for you so that you can trade freely?*

Below are some of the common answers which then emerged from various members who participated in the focused group discussion;

They should stop raiding us.
They should designate us some places where we can operate from.
They should lower their license fees because business is not good anymore.
The municipality should erect low cost trading spaces.
They must collect low cost day market fees from us.
They should allocate us some trading space then we can pay rentals on a monthly basis.
They should allocate us trading space in town.

Participants present were also asked to indicate which areas they preferred to trade in by way of raising up their hands. Interestingly, all the participants indicated that they preferred to trade in the Central Business District. Asked to give reasons and explain their choice, almost all of them indicated that, that is where urban dwellers in Marondera and surrounding areas congregate.

In trying to peacefully resolve the conflict in question, the author was of the opinion that capitalisation of vendors may be an important factor because with a strong capital base, there is sustainability. He thus sought to understand how most of them had got capitalised. More than half of the participants highlighted that they capitalised themselves through some revolving funds which are known locally as *marounds* or *mikando*. Less than half of the participants also indicated that they had capitalised themselves through own means by way of savings. Asked to explain their source of capital, the majority indicated that besides the revolving funds, they just did not have any other source of income. Most of those who said they capitalised themselves through own means explained that whilst they were still employed they made some savings or the small package that they received was quickly converted into capital.

The role of the civic society in resolving the vendor-local authority conflict

Since the author was also of the view that the civic society could play a crucial role in resolving the vendor local authority conflict in Marondera, the author posed a question to the audience intending to find out from the vendors how many of them had worked with non-governmental organisations in carrying out their business or in any related manner.

However, a small fraction said they had cooperated with some NGOs, (about 20%), they were then asked to clarify which areas exactly they had cooperated with such NGOs. They responded and said such NGOs assisted them to obtain cheap housing stands and loans which are also paid back in friendly terms. Such participants further confirmed that they conduct some annual meetings with such NGOs which however, they did not specify for ethical reasons. The author chose not to request the identity of such NGOs.

Sub-problem 2:
To what extent can citizen participation in local governance matters be promoted?

In order to address the above referred sub-problem, the author thought it wise to actually carry out some face to face interviews with a number of vendors so as to obtain first-hand information. The author assumed that in order to promote citizen participation in Marondera's local governance, some vending association can be of vital importance. Of those interviewed, 70% indicated that they were not registered with any vending association whilst only a paltry 30% indicated that they were registered with at least one vending association. Asked to explain why they were not registered with any vending association, below are some of the common answers proffered;

I have no idea at all about that.
I thought my business needs council's permission only.
I am not aware of any vending associations.
Lack of information, I don't even know of any vending association in Marondera.
No vending associations have approached us.

For the few who indicated that they were registered with at least one vending association, below are some of the reasons why they registered with such;

So that I can get good trading space.
Because we want to do vending legally.
So that we can get to know and appreciate the principles of the city of Marondera.

Furthermore, the author wanted to understand if ever the Municipality of Marondera does consult them (vendors) before embarking on any decision. This is quite an important aspect of citizen participation. Of those interviewed, 70% indicated that the municipality does not consult them whilst about 30% of the interviewees indicated that at some point in their business lifetime, the municipality has at least consulted them. The researcher probed further intending to know what the vendors think could be the reason why the municipality has not or does not consult them. Below are some of the major common responses which come from the interviewees;

they don't value our views.
they say we are not educated.
because we are operating illegally.
they take the law into their own hands.
they do not recognise us.

For those who said the municipality consulted them at some stage, below are some of their explanations;

they wanted me to carry out my business at a designated point of which I am in the process of applying for one.

they want to keep us informed so that we can make informed decisions concerning our businesses especially on how and where we should not operate from.

Sub-problem 3:
How can the vending community be persuaded to comply with the authority's regulations and by-laws

The majority of the interviewees, approximately 90% indicated that they were not registered, neither were they licenced to trade as vendors in the Central Business District. Below are some of the reasons narrated by them as to why they have such a status of unregistered/unlicensed vendors;

we have no money to spare for registration.

the licence fee is too exorbitant.

just because they don't want to see us in town.

we have not been advised how to go about the registration process.

For the few who indicated that they were registered, they said the main reason why they registered themselves was to avoid constant harassment from municipal officials. The author then solicited for some proposals or amendments which the vendors/interviewees would expect to be made on the municipal by-laws. Below are some of the proposals put forward by the vendors;

the municipality should stop raiding people.

the by-laws are tricky and old. We need new by-laws those which fit us as Zimbabwean citizens.

they should designate vendor sites which are within reach of customers

licence fees must be lowered.

vendors should be notified of any changes or developments.

the council needs to conscientise people about the registration process.

they should give vendors some vending cards so that vendors can pay some fees to the municipality on a daily basis.

the municipality should just collect fees from us from any point.

From participatory observation, in which the author disguised himself as a vendor, he realised that at any given time a vendor is not stable and does not feel safe as the raids can take place at any given time with the risk of having his wares being confiscated being very high. "Fellow vendors" also appeared not to have a keen interest at all in seeking licences neither are they willing to operate out of the Central Business District.

Sub-problem 4:
How possible is it to come up with a Marondera Municipality Vending Policy which will see a win-win situation between both conflicting parties?

To address the sub-problem, three interviews were conducted with some senior officials from the Municipality of Marondera, the Zimbabwe Chamber of Small to Medium Scale Enterprises and a non-governmental organisation operating in Marondera (name withheld).

Excerpts from an interview with Mr Nyamuziwa, Municipality of Marondera Chamber Secretary held on Thursday 14 July 2016

From several questions put across to the Municipality's Chamber Secretary, it became apparent that there was a concession to the effect that Marondera does not have a policy document specifically designed to target and regulate the issue of vending. Nevertheless, Mr Nyamuziwa made reference to the Marondera's (Hawkers and Street Vendors) By-laws, 1986. CAP 134 and the Municipality's 5 year Strategic Plan which one way or the other spell out how other stakeholders including vendors are to relate with the local authority.

Whilst the Chamber Secretary made it clear that the "illegality" of some of these vendors operating in the Central Business District was not in dispute, he however conceded that the approach or tactic they had been using of late, that of running after the vendors, which he also described as a "cat and mouse" situation had proved not to be a sustainable way at all. He explained that if anything at all, the approach has increased labour costs for the Municipality through the continuous need to increase security personnel which is supposed to deal with the illegal vendors.

From the Chamber Secretary's narration, it would appear there has been a paradigm shift in how the local authority views vendors and in how it so desires to deal with the issue of vending, explained Mr Nyamuziwa:

Since our economy is gravitating from the formal to become an informal based economy, there is a dire need for the local authority to be responsive to the needs of vendors. We need them, they are certainly contributing to the fiscus and somehow making a positive contribution to the economic development of the country at such a time. We need to allocate them some vending sites at designated points. We can also learn from the case of India and bring together other private players so that we assist each other in putting up some market stalls even in the CBD. Ours is to create a conducive environment for all stakeholders, of which the vendors are part of and also to ensure that certain health and safety standards are met,

It was then put to the Chamber Secretary that from our findings, vendors would prefer to trade in the Central Business District were human traffic is at its maximum and where business is most lucrative, but, unfortunately, it would appear the local authority at most would not tolerate that. Mr Nyamuziwa explained that it is not all about the Central Business District, but rather it is about perceptions and the need for people to change their attitudes. He gave an example of the Home Industries in Glen View, Harare which produce and sell various wooden and metal furniture items. Ordinary people from all over Zimbabwe travel to Glen View Home Industries to acquire good quality but low cost furniture, explained Mr Nyamuziwa.

Reference was also made to *Siyaso* market as well as the popular *Mupedzanhamo* market in Mbare, Harare, which has also become very common for vendors who trade in cheap clothing and other items. Travellers from all over Zimbabwe together with urban dwellers who congregate at the Mbare bus terminus create time to visit this market. The Chamber Secretary explained that all those market places are far beyond Harare's Central Business District but still a huge, lucrative market reaches them.

The Chamber Secretary also made an inference to another example within Marondera. There is a market place, which is just at the edges of the Central Business District, and it is locally known as

Mudurawall because a dura-wall (precast wall) has been erected around it. The market's vendors sell wares ranging from hardware to clothing and it is a growing market, which is actually busy during the day.

With all these examples, the Chamber Secretary explained that what is therefore called for or what is required is for vendors to establish themselves somewhere and once customers get to know of their establishment, they will pursue them as has been proved in the above cited examples referred to by the Chamber Secretary of Marondera Municipality.

During the interview, the Chamber Secretary was also asked to comment on whether the local authority does ever consults vendors before making any decision that may affect them in one way or another. Mr Nyamuziwa pointed out that in matters of local governance and as stated in their Strategic Plan, issues of stakeholder consultation and citizen participation are perceived as critically important. He went on to say that co-operation was one of the co-values of the local authority. He gave an example of budgetary consultations as another area where consultation and citizen participation is evident. In fact, Mr Nyamuziwa highlighted that these vendors do have their structures and leadership which they always meet and engage with. He went on to say that there is actually documentary proof to this effect in the form of meetings minutes for anyone who might care to verify.

Access to municipal documents

One other area which may seem to be a minor one but crucial in as far as improving citizen participation is concerned is the aspect of the local authority's visibility or accessibility by the common men such as a vendor. Efforts by the author to access the said municipal's 5 year strategic plan document and some minutes confirming citizens' (vendors') participation in council's meetings so as to verify and confirm, proved to be an upheaval task.

Case2: An interview with Mehluli Sibanda, District Chairperson for Marondera's Small to Medium Scale Enterprises held on the 14th of July 2016

Responding to questions, Mr Sibanda explained that theirs is an organisation which represents or fights for the rights of small to medium scale entrepreneurs of which vendors are part. He was also quick to make reference to a market place in Marondera town, known as *Mudurawall* which he said his organisation requested from the local authority so that traders could operate from it and their request was granted. Mr Sibanda further elaborated that currently they have successfully lobbied and were given another piece of land to establish vending sites, that which is along First Street in Marondera and in between the Police's Provincial Headquarters and OK Supermarket. Nevertheless, the author took notice of the fact that for quite some time now, this piece of land has been lying idle and not fully developed. Mr Sibanda however, explained that what has so far stalled progress is the erection of a water pipe-line and a toilet before some vending shelters can be put up.

Mr Sibanda also did not believe that this conflict or vendor-local authority debate was all about trading in the Central Business District or that distance was a major issue as he also made reference to some examples which have already been highlighted from the interview with the Chamber Secretary. He was of the opinion that it is all about perception and a need to change attitude especially on the vendors part.

Asked to comment on the approximate number of vendors in Marondera Central Business District, Mr Sibanda said that Marondera has an approximate total figure of about 500 vendors with about 300 operating in and around the Central Business district.

Asked if there is any vending policy for the town of Marondera, Mr Sibanda said he did not think there was one. He however explained that in existence is a policy framework; that which governs and regulates the operations and functions of Small to Medium Enterprises of which vendors are a part.

Case 3: An interview with Mr Zvopisa (not real name) of a certain NGO (name withheld) held on the 14th of July, 2016

Responding to questions being asked to him, Mr Zvopisa narrated that part of their core business was to ensure that the voice of citizens, vendors included, is heard. Mr Zvopisa explained that if there was any participation taking place, it was at a very low level. He blamed the council for engaging vendors or the civic society only when there is a crisis or when they need to collect some monies from them. In essence, he said there was no consultation taking place between the parties.

Mr Zvopisa also made reference to a piece of land being earmarked for vendors, that which has been referred to earlier on, which is along First Street in Marondera, between the Police Provincial Headquarters and OK Supermarket. He said not much consultation with vendors was done before earmarking such a site, which is behind the Central Business District. He suspected some political influence between the council and Zimbabwe Chamber of Small to Medium Enterprises which was also instrumental in identifying the vending site. Mr Zvopisa also bemoaned the fact that at times when they heightened their efforts of citizen participation, they are then labelled politically.

Mr Zvopisa, explaining progress made towards citizen participation said he has also been very instrumental in the formation of Marondera Progressive Residents and Ratepayers Association along the same lines, that which is also known as COMARA, and he accused it of being pro-ZANU PF political party. Mr Zvopisa said theirs was people driven.

Asked on how the civic society could help to peacefully resolve the vendor-local authority conflict Mr Zvopisa said they could help in capacity building of stakeholders or parties involved and also to continue to fight for the rights of vendors and for their voice to be heard.

Bearing in mind the two theories referred to earlier on, the community relations theory and the pyramid, it becomes apparent that it is of paramount importance to engage all parties at all the different levels in an amicable manner so as to find peaceful, long lasting solutions for a conflict.

CHAPTER 5:

CONCLUSIONS AND RECOMMENDATIONS

The ever rising cost of fighting vending in the Central Business Districts

An official with the Municipality of Marondera conceded that fighting vendors was costly to the council through increased recruitment of municipal police officers. With such evidence it becomes manifestly clear that continuously fighting off vendors using municipal police is not a sustainable measure at all which could at least help manage the conflict existing between vendors and the local authority in Marondera. Instead of the measure helping boost municipal revenue, it is unnecessarily drawing from its coffers through increased labour costs which after all are not helping to alleviate the situation. This actually turned to be the similar case with the City of Kumasi wherein it was discovered that the amount of money spent on security personnel and other members of the demolition teams was high and could not be maintained (Ayeh, Emefa, Sylvana and Isaac, 2009).

During a participatory observation, the author realised that during sporadic raids of vendors in Marondera's town, the municipal police took centre stage. With the municipal "police" being involved, the impression which is given would be that they are dealing with criminals of a violent disposition. Could this be the position of the whole matter? The answer is in the negative. The situation at hand is that of a people who solely have vending as their source of living. They are contending for a lucrative trading space and the most unfortunate thing is that they have hinged their hopes on the Central Business District as they hope that it is a life time solution to their life problems. Therefore, unleashing the municipal police on such a people may not yield the intended results and this then brings one to question of the sustainability of such a "municipal police" approach. Mitullah (2003) had also castigated local authorities' efforts to address vendor-local authority conflicts by placing management of such crises in the hands of wrong departments.

In this regard, Mitullah (2003) proposed that it would actually be better to entrust the social services departments or revenue departments with the management of the vendor-local authority conflict because such departments would appreciate better the socio-economic and political background of street vending hence increasing chances of finding sustainable measures of resolving such a conflict. This therefore exposes a gap that exists between what other local authorities globally have done to deal with the vending issue and that which the town of Marondera has been doing.

Various approaches of dealing with the vendor crisis

If what was said by the majority of vendors in the town of Marondera is anything to go by, then the Municipality of Marondera can also not be exonerated from allegations of relying on a bulldozer approach as a way of dealing with the Central Business District's vending community. Many complained that they have lived with municipal raids which invariably can unexpectedly take place on an hourly, daily, weekly, monthly or once in a while basis. Some scholars have described this as a fire fighting approach that which only reacts after an incident.

A representative of a certain other Non-Governmental Organisation operating in Marondera also confirmed the "fire-fighting" approach of the Municipality of Marondera when he said the local authority would only engage them or the vendors only if the crisis escalates or if they expect or want some revenue from them. If such complaints against the municipality are true, then such measures or approaches to deal with such a conflict are not sustainable in anyway. To prove this, despite such measures, the vendor-local authority conflict has always been recurring and at times growing in scale.

Nevertheless, from the findings of this study, it does not appear as if the Municipality of Marondera still harbours hopes of achieving its goals through the bulldozer or fire-fighting approach. In an interview with the municipality's Chamber Secretary, it came out clear that the Municipality of Marondera has reached a point where they have realised that both vendors and the local authority need each other. The Chamber secretary also indicated that some efforts have been made and some are still underway, especially to allocate vendors legitimate trading space. Mr Mehluli Sibanda, the District Chairperson of Zimbabwe Chamber of Small to Medium Scale Enterprises also confirmed this as he said, in conjunction with the municipality of Marondera, they have at least managed to secure some vending sites such as the *Durawall market* and another yet to be functional along First Street. Commenting on city vending in Kumasi, Ghana, Ayeh, et al., (2009) condemned what they termed the bulldozer approach which at times is adopted by Kumasi City authorities as they attempt to destroy some vending structures. It is quite encouraging to learn that when Kumasi City fathers decide to carry out a city decongestion exercise, they issue a notice of eviction with a two week deadline. This appears more human and conscious of human rights and the Municipality of Marondera can surely draw some lessons out of that.

The role of the civic society in resolving the vendor-local authority conflict

Although the author quickly grasped that in Marondera there could be at least two associations or members of the civic society which one way or the other deals with vendors, it was then surprising to discover that about 70% of the vending population were not registered with any of the organisations. The majority further indicated that they were not even aware neither did they have any information about vending associations in Marondera. This becomes testimony of the fact that the existing associations or organisations lack the zest, zeal and the drive to mobilise and organise vendors. They remain unknown, operating underground, only to surface and become visible when there appears to be some form of benefit for someone.

With a weak civic society, it means no positive pressure is mounted on the local government. No watchdog role is played. Its mediation role is not fulfilled. It also translate to say there is not much capacity building taking place both on the vendors' side and on the municipality's side. With such a void, chances are very high that the conflict may still exist for a while unabated.

Of the 30% which indicated that they were at least affiliated with a vending association, it was clear that most of them did so for quite noble reasons. It was their hope that such associations would be able to help them acquire good trading space, they thought through such associations they could have vending legalised in the practical sense and they also hoped that they could be assisted to get low cost housing. Unfortunately, with a weak civic society in Marondera, doors have thus been opened for politicians who at most are capitalising on such a gap as they pretend to represent vendors. Such representation is however on a seasonal basis, especially when general elections are around the corner.

Although Cheema (2011) is of the opinion that in urban areas Non-Governmental Organisations have played a major role over the years in urban shelter, services and protecting interests of slum dwellers and squatters, there is no doubt that in this regard, a serious gap exists as Marondera lacks a vibrant, active civic society which could be very instrumental in dealing with the vendor-local authority conflict.

The Central Business District being a lucrative trading space debate

In as far as exploring sustainable measures of resolving the vendor-local authority conflict in Marondera is concerned, there has been an **emerging trend**, especially as propounded by the local authority and also supported by the Zimbabwe Chamber of Small to Medium Scale Entrepreneurs, that is to say, the whole issue is not about the Central Business District but about vendors getting established somewhere at which customers can then come for them.

Such a school of thought knocked some sense especially as reference was made to some thriving markets in Zimbabwe such as *mbare musika, mupedzanhamo market, siyaso market, durawall market* and *kuGlenview,* just to mention but a few, all of which are miles away from the capital city's Central Business District. All the same, it is not an overnight thing to try and deconstruct the mind's configurations of customers and vendors and try to convince them that there is also life beyond the Central Business District. This would therefore call for some interim sustainable measures to be explored.

However, several related studies also seemed to suggest that the Central Business district happens to be the only prime trading space from which vendors could operate (Brown, 2006). The logic behind such reasoning is premised on the view that it is in the Central Business District that many people from all walks of life converge for business and hence offers the best market.

Voice of vendors in urban planning

In the case of Marondera, from the survey, there were not any indications to suggest anything of that sort ever took place between vendors and the town's urban planners. Roever (2010) had agitated for the inclusion of the voice of vendors at the stage of urban planning. This would mean that urban planners and city architects would engage vendors and take note of their proposals whilst they also knock sense into them. This would then culminate into a negotiation of mutual vending sites such that vendors would appreciate why they have been allocated certain sites and why not certain sites. This therefore further exposes another gap which the Municipality of Marondera may need to fill if sustainable measures of resolving the vendor-local authority conflict in Marondera are to be realised.

The sustainability of vending machines

I am not in dispute that vending has not been a menace in most of the First World Cities as it has been in African cities. This is owing to the fact that in First World Cities, there has also been an intense use of vending machines. In a way, they help decongest a city and in this era of technological advancement, their potential in resolving a vendor-local authority conflict may not be underestimated but rather, there might be a need to experiment with them. In the case of Marondera, there has not been any evidence of anyone contemplating the use of vending machines in the town.

However, it is the sustainability part of it which may pose a dichotomy as to whether the use of vending machine may provide the much needed solution to the conflict at hand. If vending machines are to be adopted, that may mean drastically cutting off the number of vendors in town. That will impact negatively on people's lives, the majority of whom solely rely on vending. On the other hand, although vending machines may spell a good fortune, revenue wise, they are capital intense. That will also mean that the municipality will have a monopoly of trade which is quite unfair, unless it decides to rent such to other players. If street vendors manage to get established somewhere as has been the case with some other thriving vendor markets referred to earlier on then the local authority may proceed to also have vending machines in the Central Business District and at the end of the day it may be a win-win situation for all the concerned parties. Vending machines may not need to be implemented in isolation but in conjunction with other measures so as to have a sustainable solution to the conflict in question.

Formalization of vending

It has been demonstrated that one other key contributory factor to the vendor-local authority conflict globally is the informality and the illegality status that is attributed to street vending (Mitullar 2003, Anetor 2015, Broomley 2000, Njaya 2014 and Roever 2005). This therefore means that a sustainable measure aimed at resolving any vendor-local authority conflict in Marondera should be gravitating towards improving such a derogatory status of vendors so that in the end, a win-win situation for both conflicting parties is established. In the case of Marondera, although vending has not been explicitly outlawed several bottlenecks, by-laws and the conduct of municipal authorities have made it difficult for vendors to freely trade. There is a dire need to visit all these as a way of formalising vending in Marondera so that it can be sustainable and hence resolve the conflict. Probably this can be done by way of coming up with a vending policy which is tailor-made for vendors.

Vending policy

Coming up with a policy document (and its implementation) is one serious way of which the government through local authorities can show its commitment to effectively address the vending crisis. It has been demonstrated that most First World Countries and some Asian countries do have some vending policies those which govern and regulate the operations of vendors in all aspects, in areas under their jurisdiction. The Municipality of Marondera Chamber Secretary made a concession that although they have a Strategic Plan which also partly encompasses vending, there was no vending policy in Marondera. Mr Mehluli Sibanda, the District Chairperson of the Zimbabwe Chamber of Small to Medium Scale Entrepreneurs also confirmed the same position when he said that besides a policy document for Small to Medium Scale Enterprises, which also partly covers vending, there was no actual policy on vending in Marondera and this further exposes another serious gap which may need to be filled up as a matter of urgency.

The importance of citizen participation has been emphasized through various related literature. During the data gathering process, it was quite interesting that when the research population was asked if they were participating in local governance matters which affect their day to day lives one way or the other. Almost every stakeholder interviewed on the same subject proffered some answers which differed from those which were proffered by others thereby leaving the author wondering if all these stakeholders were commenting on the same subject of citizen participation in the jurisdiction of Marondera Municipality or not, or rather, it could be that the parties concerned in this conflict understood citizen participation from different perspectives and dimensions.

According to text *narrative 1*, the Chamber Secretary for the Municipality of Marondera indicated that in his council, citizen/stakeholder participation was of crucial and primary importance. He highlighted that there was a lot of citizen participation taking place through efforts such as budget consultation, meetings, just to mention but a few. Mr Nyamuziwa actually bragged that there was documentary proof to that effect in the form of minutes which are filed.

Nevertheless, contrary to what the Chamber Secretary was saying, it emerged from text **narrative 3**, as argued by a representative of a certain Non-Governmental Organisation in Marondera that if at all, vendor consultation was at minimum levels but that vendors or the civic society are consulted only when there appears to be a need. Vendors were also asked the same question concerning their participation in local governance and they complained that the Municipality of Marondera does not consult them. They further speculated that the reasons could be that the Municipality of Marondera does not value their views, they were deemed not educated, and that they are said to be operating illegally hence not recognised. It was only Mr Sibanda of the Zimbabwe Chamber of Small to Medium Scale Entrepreneurs who confirmed that his organisation has also worked in consultation with the municipality and he was quiet grateful that most of the meetings were fruitful. This was according to the findings from text *narrative 2*.

The above scenario demonstrates another **emerging trend** that there is a willingness and goodwill amongst all the conflicting parties to work together with the hope of addressing the issue at hand had it not be for certain impediment which this book also seek to expose. What is more evident is that there is a general mistrust amongst all the stakeholders. There is finger pointing and blame shift with each stakeholder believing that he/she has already done the best which he/she could and that it is now up to the other conflicting party(s) to either comply or to play its part. It is a blame shift game. The municipality is satisfied with the level of citizen participation in town. The Zimbabwe Chamber of Small to Medium Scale Entrepreneurs is in agreement with that position whilst the civic society and vendors feel otherwise. This calls for initiatives which can effectively bring all the conflicting parties to a round table for a sustainable dialogue so that if possible, a taskforce can be commissioned to ensure that the resolutions of their meetings are implemented. The task force should have all the stakeholders' representatives.

Compliance with by-laws

In as far as compliance with by-laws is concerned, particularly the payment of registration fees and taxes concerned, a striking difference was noted between the jurisdiction of the Municipality of Marondera and that of Kumasi in Ghana. Whilst it was established that the majority of vendors in Kumasi were indeed paying taxes (Ayeh et al 2009), it came out from the study that about 90% of the street vending population in Marondera Central District was not registered, and neither did they pay anything to the municipality. During interviews, various reasons were put forward for such non-compliance. The majority of them indicated that they had no money to spare for registration. This comes as a no surprise especially at this point in time when the economy is not performing well. The little they get is quickly converted for survival. The importance of paying taxes to the municipality is not known neither are the advantages of doing so being seen since it is also not in dispute that service provision is also at a decline.

For those who may wish to register with the Municipality of Marondera, the license of $100 per annum has proved to be exorbitant for vendors who cannot afford to pay it at once. However, if lessons are to be learnt from the case of Kumasi in Ghana, it is quite pleasing to learn that at least 75% of vendors do pay some revenue to the local authority. The City of Kumasi accepts fees on a daily or monthly basis. It is also important to recall that from the data gathering many vendors in Marondera so wished that the municipality may collect fees from them on a daily basis. This will also mean that the payment rate or the fee per day would come down to affordable level of even a dollar or less, something which vendors would manage.

The City of Kumasi does have its own revenue collecting officers but what David, Ulrich, Zelzek and Majoe (2009) advocated for, that is to delegate the management of certain vending sites or markets to vendors themselves can be explored as a sustainable measure of resolving the vendor-local authority conflict in Marondera. It is therefore emphasized that if this is properly done, vendors will become their own police thereby grooming a sense of responsibility and there will be increased tax collections on the part of the local authority. The same was implemented in Bamako, Mali and not only did it see an increase in revenue collection but also an improvement in the working environment of the vendors.

Most local authorities would not tolerate vendors operating in front of other people's shop pavements. Despite this, the majority of vendors particularly in African cities have continued to defy such by-laws and operate just on the pavements of other taxpaying people's shops. Kumasi introduced a 1% fee which is extended to such affected shop owners and this becomes a regulatory measure, which is in a way sustainable as it offers a win-win situation for the local authority, vendors and shop owners. Such is a measure which the Municipality of Marondera has not yet explored.

In as far as the Marondera's Hawkers and Street Vendors By-Laws are concerned, it is apparent that the majority of vendors did not know about them as a paltry number of less than 10% only made reference to this particular set of by-laws. It would appear as if their compliance with the by-laws, if at all, is based on conscience or tenets of natural justice and on the other hand, their failure to comply with the same set of rules could be based on ignorance of the laws. This is so especially when taking into account that some respondents indicated that they just did not know the requirements of how to go about the registration process.

Furthermore, as obtained from the data gathering process, one respondent indicated that Marondera Municipality Vending By-laws were quite tricky and old. He indicated that they would want some fresh ones which fit a Zimbabwean society. Indeed there is no doubt

74

that the currently operating vending by-laws are quite old, having been enacted or repealed in 1986. Society is dynamic and there might be a genuine need to re-visit the by-laws with the intention of seeing if they are still applicable to the town of Marondera of 2016 as they were applied to the same town, just six years after the country obtained its independence.

Section 7 and Section 8 of these by-laws stipulates the cancellation of registration certificates for ex-convicts. These could be the other things which are repelling some vendors from coming forward to register. There is no doubt that some people who trade as vendors are ex-convicts, hence by-laws of any city or town are bound to reflect principles of restorative justice as opposed to retributive justice which is merely punitive and not sustainable.

Nevertheless, a close scrutiny of the content of the by-laws in question would indicate that the majority of laid down rules and procedures are actually in the best interest of public health and security so as to promote peace and order and also avert pandemics which can quickly spread like veldt fires if vending is not regulated and that would mean that a complete overhaul of the by-laws of Marondera may not be called for. Such calls have at most been made by people who are of the opinion that the current set of by-laws are a reflection of the colonial master's evil intentions upon the black majority. However, a comparison of the same by-laws with those of the City of Cambridge Outdoor Vendors By-Law #106-09 (2009) would indicate that the later, although being recent, are stiffer and stricter than those found in most African Cities and towns.

Probably, this explains why there is so much order in European cities and why vending has not been much of a crisis as it has been on our side. However, caution has to be exercised against adopting what cities like Cambridge have done on African soil, particularly

75

Sub- Sahara. Our socio-economic and political background differs a lot. Whilst in Europe the economy is not informal and whilst the majority there do not depend on vending as their only source of living, the opposite is quite true in the case of Marondera. The point in question is the argument of Marondera Vending by-laws being colonial in nature falls off as they are more or less the same with those of eThekwini Municipality, South Africa (2014) which is a thriving South African local authority. It is apparent that its goals and objectives are equally in the best interest of public health, peace, order and security.

Social protection for vendors

About 80% of vendors in and around the Central Business District indicated that they did not have any social security of some sort. The small percentages of those affiliated to pension, medical aid and funeral policies can possibly be attributed to people who have been previously employed before getting retrenched or retiring and were on a pension scheme hence being able to continue catering for medical and funeral policies. Another fraction could also be attributed to those who have been secured as dependents of other people who are formally employed. Also note that it emerged that none is subscribing to any educational policy as this has turned out to be a luxury.

Social security has remained a pipe dream for vendors as the economy does not allow them to save towards all that. They survive on a hand to mouth basis. Others who had previously insured themselves were affected by the change of currency in Zimbabwe from the Zimbabwean dollar to a multi-currency system and now the so-called bond notes, and because generally, the economy is not performing well. All the same, this cannot be an excuse for the vending population in Marondera to be left vulnerable and exposed to the uncertainties of life or of the future like that. They need assistance on how best they can get themselves organized and get insured in a viable and sustainable manner, taking into account their circumstances. Insurance schemes have to be tailor-made, those which fit the informal trader.

Social protection for vendors is something which very few governments, if any have taken very seriously thereby leaving vendors and those who depend on them vulnerable and exposed to an unsecured and uncertain future. Even for certain American cities such as Lima and Peru, only less than 20% of the street vendors are enrolled in a pension scheme and are affiliated with a health care system (Roever, 2010). Also in India, there has been very few street vending associations such as the Self Employed Women's Association of India which have managed to sustain group insurance. The whole idea is that of ensuring a win-win situation for all particularly ensuring that vending becomes viable and sustainable not only economically but socially as well instead of being a menace as is the current situation. The same can also be said about the opening or the creation of credit lines for vendors.

Credit lines for vendors

If Zimbabwe as a nation requires financial credit lines from the Bretton Woods Institutions; the International Monetary Fund and the World Bank, how much more would the informal traders, particularly vendors in Marondera be in need of financial support in form of credit lines, as a sustainable measure of resolving the vendor-local authority impasse. Such funds would mainly be for re-capitalization. Mitullah (2003) bemoaned the fact that financing of street vendors is non-existent at all and if ever it becomes available, the interest rates are as high as 20%. This is also what turned out to be the case in the situation of Marondera.

Due to a lack of collateral, vendors cannot easily get a cheap loan at any financial institutions like banks. This leaves Marondera vendors at the mercy of dubious micro-financial institutions and individuals whose interest rates are exorbitant and continue to accrue on the balance on a monthly basis, a practice known locally as *chimbadzo*. Politicians have also capitalized on the situation. During election time, they bring forward what is commonly referred to as *projects money* which at most is distributed by the well connected on partisan lines, meaning to say the risk of political opponents not benefiting is very high. Besides that, the disbursed amounts of money may not be sufficient. The loans are not supported by monitoring, evaluation and implementation or technical advice and as a result, in most cases, abuse of funds, diversion of funds, and payment defaults are common such that the fund has no continuity. The rest of the people will eventually not benefit, maybe up until the next election period. As it emerged from the findings, the majority of vendors in Marondera have now resorted to own means of capitalizing themselves especially through what has come to be known as revolving finds (*mikando/maround*).

Nevertheless, such a gap needs to be filled by also drawing some lessons from the Kenyan case whereby at the time, (Mitullah, 2003) there were suggestions of an establishment of a Micro-Entrepreneurs Bank, that which was going to specifically target and help informal traders including vendors by availing loans to small to medium scale entrepreneurs at reasonable rates. In Kumasi, Ghana once again, Ayeh et al (2009) spoke of soft loans which are disbursed to vendors and payable within a three months period. Furthermore, vendors in Kumasi, Ghana, do have the option and privilege of purchasing perishable goods meant for resale on credit and then pay later at the end of the day. The Arusha local government (Tanzania) as well has since ceased to perform arbitrary evictions on vendors but rather they support the informal sector with loans (David et al, 2009).

Such measures, if also adopted by the vendors and the Municipality of Marondera would certainly prove to be sustainable measures which can help resolve the vendor-local authority conflict in question. It is the prerogative of the municipality to put in place such mechanisms since it is the one which has the means, the capacity and the expertise to spearhead all these initiatives compared to vendors.

Demographic data

The findings of this study also revealed that men slightly out-numbered women at a ratio of 60:40, being vendors operating in Marondera's Central Business District. There is no doubt that this can be linked to a patriarchal system which characterizes our society whereupon it is generally believed that it is the man who should go out and fend for the family. The 40% of women vendors may be comprising of those women who have now taken heed of the recent gospel of gender equity, equality and women empowerment, that is to say women are also equal partners with men, that they can also do it and that they can also fend for themselves and for their families some of which they singlehandedly head. Through the Domestic Violence Act enacted as an Act of Parliament in 2007, women can now get protection orders (peace order like) from courts which protect them also from any form of economic abuse. More so, the other reason could be that the majority of women are found at the rural side taking part in some form of farming activities one way or the other, but sadly, the majority of them do not own the land which they till. A bid to find sustainable measure of resolving the vendor local authority conflict might have to bear all this information in mind, especially from a gender perspective.

A look at age groups which operate in the Central Business District of Marondera would indicate that the local authority and the central government cannot afford to turn a blind eye to this vendor-local authority conflict as the majority of vendors are aged between 19-39 years. That is about 85% of the total street vending population. This is the economically active group of the country and if they are not properly considered and supported or if they are carelessly frustrated, it is the national economy which at the end of the day suffers. All the other age groups one way or the other depend on this particular age group as it turned out from the survey that most people between the 19-39 years age group have an average of at least 3 dependents living under their roofs.

The educational levels of the respondents, as it emerged from the distributed questionnaires indicate there is no doubt that Zimbabwe is indeed a highly literate nation. Almost all vendors went beyond basic primary education (Grade 7). About more than half of the street vending population reached Ordinary Level. About 20% went through Advanced Level and about 10% are degreed. This means that the vendors in question are quite literate to be taught and be able to grasp business management concepts. They can also be helped to get organized in a much better manner. All they need is a well-coordinated effort.

When setting up license and registration fees and in order to come up with sustainable measures, the Municipality of Marondera may need to take into account the monthly average incomes for street vendors in the Central Business District and if this is considered it can also go a long way in ensuring maximum compliance with some of these requirements and by-laws. The majority of vendors, about 60% of them, do get an average profit of $100 per month. Obviously they do have basic needs to take care of such as decent accommodation, transport, decent clothing, food, basic education and basic health care. Trying to imagine them prioritizing the payment of $100 license fee, though per annum, but at once can be ill-conceived.

Major findings of the study

- Sporadic raids on vendors by municipal polices are still taking place
- Vendors are willing to be designated reasonable places to operate from
- The registration/license fee is beyond reach of many vendors
- Almost all vendors prefer to trade in the Central Business District
- However, the success of vending is not only limited to trading in the Central Business District
- There are no reliable credit lines for vendors in Marondera
- The majority of street vendors, about 80% of them do not have any form of social security
- 70% of the street vendors indicated that the municipality of Marondera does not or did not consult them before making any major decision which affects them, meaning citizen participation is very low
- There is no vendor policy for the town of Marondera

81

- Although the by-laws need to be refreshed, they are not the root cause of the conflict

Conclusions

- There is a serious mistrust, lack of coordination and cooperation amongst vendors and the local authority and this has seen an escalation of the conflict
- There is an absence of a strong, effective and vibrant civic society in Marondera, that which can help resolve the conflict in question skillfully through playing a mediation role
- Vendors in Marondera are a vulnerable specie, without social security, financial or technical support and they are operating at the mercy of the local authority

Recommendations

Based on the findings of the study, the following are recommended; There is an urgent need to adopt a third party intervention initiative in this vendor-local authority conflict. Such should be a mediator with high conflict resolution and negotiation skills. It is further proposed that such a role can be fulfilled by an effective neutral and independent civic society. The use of a prominent, respectable person may also not be ruled out.

Citizenry participation should be heightened up by way of ensuring that vendors are represented in all decision making meetings and boards. Their voice should be heard and must count. During urban and town planning vendors need to be consulted and contribute. To consult them or their leaders only at budgeting stage is not enough.

There is a need to help establish strong effective civic society groups which shall continue to fight for the recognition and for the rights of vendors so that they are not at the mercy of anyone.

In this regard, vendors need to be assisted so that they get organized and establish some vendors' associations which amongst other things will speak on their behalf. Such currently existing associations or organizations need to boost up their membership recruitment drive and become vibrant in fulfilling their mandate.

A three tier task force, comprising of vendors, the Municipality of Marondera and the civic society needs to be set up to ensure that all issues to do with vending and local governance are well coordinated, well implemented, well monitored and well evaluated so that mutual cooperation, trust and confidence building is achieved.

The task force should go ahead and draft a vendor's policy for the Municipality of Marondera that which will exhaust all issues of interest, difficulty and concern in as far as vending is concerned.

The task force should seek government assistance to establish an Entrepreneurs Bank of Marondera through which vendors can access cheap soft loans with favorable terms and conditions so as to re-capitalize vendors.

The task force needs to design some social security schemes which are tailor-made for street traders, those to which they can contribute smaller amounts and intervals whilst their funds are invested and managed elsewhere.

The municipality may explore the use vending machines as a way of decongesting the town.

The municipality should consider delegating the management of vendors and vending markets to vendors themselves.

The municipality should consider collecting the lowered fees at least on a daily basis.

References

Anetor, F. O. (2015).*An Investigation Into The Value of Street Vending in Nigeria: A Case of Lagos State.Journal of Marketing and Consumer Research.* Vol. 11. 2015.

Ayeh, S, Emefa, B, Sylvana, K. R and Isaac, D. N. (2009).*Street Vending and the Use of Public Space in Kumasi, Ghana.*

Bolarinwa, J. O. (2006). PCR 702: *Research Methods in Peace and Conflict Resolution.* Lagos. National Open University of Nigeria.

Brown, A. (2004). *"Cities for the Urban Poor in Zimbabwe: Urban Space as a Resource for Sustainable Development",* In Westerndorff, D and Eade, D, *Development and Cities,* (eds). Oxford. Oxfarm GB.

Brown, T. L, Potoski, M, and Slyke, D. M. (2007).*Trust and Contract Completeness in the Public Sector.* Local Government Studies, 33:4, 607-623   http://dx.doi.org/10.1080/03003930701417650   visited 23/03/16.

Cheema, G. S. (2011).*Engaging Civil Society to Promote Democratic Local Governance: Emerging Trends and Policy Implications in Asia.* Working Paper No. 7. Visby. Swedish International Centre for Local Democracy. *Conflict Management and Resolution.* Centre for Multi-Party Democracy, Malawi.

David, S, Ulrich, O, Zelezeck, S and Majoe, N. (2009).*Managing Informality: Local Government Practices and Approaches towards the Informal Economy.* Learning examples from five countries. Pretoria. A Collaborative Initiative of the South Africa LED Network/ SALGA AND LEDNA.

Dodo, O, Chideya, T, Chawanza, Z. (2010).*Peace, Gender and Conflict Resolution.* Mount Pleasant. Harare. Zimbabwe Open University.

Dodo, O and Chiwanza, K. (2011). *Ethics of Peace and Conflict Management*. Mt Pleasant. Zimbabwe Open University.

Dodo, O and Mateura, Z. (2011). *Governance, Participation and Human Rights*. Mt Pleasant, Zimbabwe Open University.

Dube, D and Chirisa, I. (2012). *The Informal City; Assessing Its Scope, Variants and Direction in Harare, Zimbabwe*. Global Advanced Research Journal of Geography and Regional Planning. Vol. 1(1) pp016-025, May 2012. *eThekwini Municipality: Informal Trading By-Law, 2014*.

Fisher, S, Abdi, D. I, Ludin, J, Smith, R, Williams, S AND Sue, W. (2000). *Working With Conflict. Skills and Strategies for Action*. London. Zed Books.

Gaventa, J and Valderrama, C, *Participation, Citizenship and Local Governance*. Background notes Prepared for Washington on Strengthening Participation in Local Governance. Institute of Development Studies, June 21-24, 1999.

Gutsa, I, Dodo, O, Mutsau, S, M. T, Hlatywayo, L, and Majoni, C. (2011).*Peace Education and Media*. MSPL 514.Mt Pleasant. Zimbabwe Open University.

Haralambos, M and Holban, M. C (1990) *Social Themes Perspectives*. London. Clay Limited.

Healthy Vending Machine Policy of March 2006. County of San Diego Department of Parks and Recreation www.goplayetfit.com www.sdunnonline.org visited 31/05/16.

IEMS- Informal Economy Monitoring Study. *Ahmedabad's Street Vendors: Realities and Recommendations. Increasing Citizen Participation in Local Governance:* Latin Americas' Local Citizen Councilshttp://ella.practicalaction.org/visited 23/03/16marine@fundar.org.mx visited 23/03/16.

86

Jick, T. D. (1979).*Process and Impacts of a Merger: Individuals Organisation Perspectives*. Doctoral Dissertation. New York State School of Industrial and Labour Relations. Cornwell University.

Jick, T. D. *Mixing Qualitative and Quantitative Methods. Triangulation in Action*. Cornwell University. December 1979. Vol. 24.

Jongh, L. (2015). *"Street Vending in Urban Malawi: Strategies and Practices of Vendors and Local Authorities"*. Paper presented at the RC21 International Conference on *"The ideal City: Between myth and reality. Representations, Policies, Contradictions and Challenges for tomorrow's Urban Life"*. Urbino (Italy) 27-29 August http//www.rczi.org/en/conferences/urbino2015 visited 13/03/2016.

Klein, H, *the Right to Political Participation and the Information Society*. Presented at Global Democracy Conference, Montreal, May 29-June 1, 2005.

Kusakabe, K. (2006).*Policy Issues on Street Vending: An Overview of Studies in Thailand, Cambodia and Mongolia*. International Labour Organisation.

Lanre Olaolu, Amodu (undated) *Community Relations Strategies and Conflict Resolution in the Niger Delta: A study of three major oil companies,* A thesis in the Department of Mass Communication submitted to the College of Development Studies in Partial fulfilment of the Requirements for the Award of the Degree of Doctor of Philosophy, of Covenant University, Ota, Ogun State, Nigeria

Marondera (Hawkers and Street Vendors) By-Laws, 1986. Cap134.

McMillan, J. (1989).*Research in Education. A Conceptual Introduction.* Harper and Collins.

Mealey, L. (2009).*Healthy Vending Guide*Nemours Health and Prevention Services www.nemours.org/growuphealthy.com visited 28/05/16.

Meldon, J, Walsh. J and Kenny. M. (2000).*Local Governance, Local Development and Citizen Participation*. Lessons from Ireland.

Mitullah, W. V. *Street Vending in African Cities; A Synthesis of Empirical Findings from Kenya, Cote D' Ivore, Ghana, Zimbabwe, Uganda and South Africa*. Background Paper for 2005 World Development Report. 16th of August 2003.

Mohammaddi, S. H, Norazizan. S and Shahvandi. A. R (2011) *Civic Engagement, Citizen Participation and Quality of Governance in Iran*. Journal of Human Ecology, 36(3):211-216. Kamla-Raj.

Musingafi, M. M. C and Hlatywayo, L. (2013).*Research Methods*. Mt Pleasant. Zimbabwe Open University.

Mutsetse, P. (2015).*An Evaluation of the Accessibility of HIV and AIDS Related Information Among People With Hearing Impairments In Marondera District Peri- Urban Colleges*, A Research Project Submitted In Partial Fulfilment of the Requirement for the Master's Degree in Special Education. Harare. Zimbabwe Open University.

Njaya, T. (2014).*Challenges of Negotiating Sectorial Governance of Street Vending Sector in Harare Metropolitan, Zimbabwe*. Asian Journal of Economic Modelling, 2014, 2(2): 69-84. http://www.aessweb.com/journals/5009visited 23/03/16.

Promoting People's Participation and Governance in Vietnamese Cities Through the Association of Cities in Vietnam, (ACVN). People's Participation and Local Governance. Challenges and Opportunities. Konrad. Adenauer-Stiftung ev and the Association of Cities of Vietnam.

Ritchie, J and Lewis, J. (2003).*A Guide for Social Science Students and Researchers*. London, Sage Publications. New Delhi, The Oaks.

Roever, S. (2010). *"Street Trade in Latin America: Demographic Trends, Legal Issues and Vending Organisations in Six Countries"* in Bhowmik, S, ed, *Street Vendors in the Global Economy*. New Delhi. Routledge.

Roth, C. (2003). (eds) *Conflict Sensitive Approach to Humanitarian Assistance and Peace Building Tools for Peace and Conflict.*

Sarmiento, H. (2015).*The Spatial Politics of Street Vending in Loa Angeles.* Research and Policy Brief. Number 19. Los Angeles UCLA Institute for Research on Labour and Employment.

Skinner, C. (2008).*Street Trade in Africa: A Review.* School of Development Studies. Working Paper No. 51. University of Kwazulu Natal.

The Herald, Tuesday 17 November 2015. Harare. Zimbabwe Papers.

Walsh, J. (2000).*Street Vendors and the Dynamics of the Informal Economy; Evidence from Vung Tau, Vietnam.* Asian Social Science Journal. Vol 6. No. 11.

Willemse, L. (2009).*Opportunities and Constraints Facing Informal Street Traders.* Evidence from South African Cities.

www.why.do/wp-content/uploads/2013/06/why-do-cats-chase-mice.jpg

www.newsdzezimbabwe.co.uk/2016/02/council-u-turns-on-mbare-evictions.html?m=1Accessed 17/02/17

www.newzimbabwe.com/news-30218-teargas+as+cops+break+demo,+arrest+vendors/news.aspxAccessed 15/7/17

www.newzimbabwe.com/news-3976-mugabe+vendors+war+illegal+global+union/news.aspx Accessed 23/10/17

www.newsdzezimbabwe.co.uk/2016/02/1-500-mbare-traders-face-eviction.html?m=1 Accessed 14/02/17

www.newsdzezimbabwe.co.uk/2017/11/we-will-drive-out-vendors-hre-council.html?m=1 Accessed 27/11/17

Yin, R. K. (2011).*Qualitative Research from Start to Finish.* New York and London. The Guilford Press.

Universal Declaration of Human Rights (1948).

Zanna, A. S. (2015).*Citizen Participation in Local Governance and Sustainability of Programmes*. Global Journal of Science Frontier Research: E Inter- disciplinary. Volume 15. Issue 3. Version 1.0. Type: Double Blind. Peer Reviewed International Research Journal. Global Journals Inc. (USA).

APPENDIX 1

MUNICIPALITY OF MARONDERA

MUNICIPAL OFFICES 24941/2/3, 21801-8
FAX 24944, TELEX 81032
DOMBOTOMBO OFFICES 23106, 24166
NYAMENI OFFICES 24550
All communications to be
addressed to the Town Clerk

MUNICIPAL OFFICES

P.O. BOX 261

MARONDERA

Your Ref_____

ZIMBABWE

Our Ref March 2016_____

BRUNO SHORA
2190 BOTEREKWA
CHERUTOMBO
MARONDERA

Ref: **APPLICATION FOR PERMISSION TO CARRY OUT A RESEARCH IN AND AROUND THE CENTRAL BUSINESS DISTRICT**

We write to advise that permission has been granted for you to carry out the study in our jurisdiction with a hope of exploring sustainable measures of dealing with the vendor-local authority conflict. We hope at the end of the study, you will furnish us with a copy of your study for analysis of the outcome and also for consideration of your recommendations.

Thank you.

Yours faithful

R Nyamuziwa

Chamber Secretary

For: Town Clerk/ Chief Executive

Municipality of Marondera
CHAMBER SECRETARY

1 8 MAR 2016

P.O BOX 261, MARONDERA
TEL:(0279) 23917, 24941/2

92

APPENDIX 2

ZRP MARONDERA CENTRAL

BOX 88

MARONDERA

22 FEBRUARY 2016

BRUNO SHONA

REF : NOTIFICATION OF INTENT TO CARRYOUT SOME SURVEYS IN AND AROUND MARONERA CBD.

1. Reference is made to the above matter.

2. I acknowledge receipt of your notification letter dated 15 February 2016.

3. Please be advised that Police can not authorize you or deny you to carryout such surveys since it is an individual programme .

Signed ....Chief Inspector Jokonya

(Officer In-Charge Marondera Central)